Practicing Judicious Discipline:

An Educator's Guide
to a Democratic Classroom

Fourth Edition
Revised, Expanded, and Updated

Edited by Barbara Landau

Caddo Gap Press

Practicing Judicious Discipline:
An Educator's Guide to a Democratic Classroom

Edited by Barbara Landau

Fourth Edition, 2008
Revised, Expanded, and Updated

Third Edition, 1999
Second Edition, 1994
First Edition, 1991

Published by:
Caddo Gap Press
3145 Geary Boulevard, PMB 275
San Francisco, California 94118, U.S.A.

ISBN 1-880192-54-3

Price $29.95 US

Cover Drawing by Brynn Lawler

Library of Congress Cataloging-in-Publication Data

Practicing judicious discipline : an educator's guide to a democratic classroom / edited by Barbara Landau. — 4th ed. revised, expanded, and updated.
     p. cm.
  ISBN 1-880192-54-3 (alk. paper)
  1. School discipline—Handbooks, manuals, etc. 2. Classroom management—Handbooks, manuals, etc. I. Landau, Barbara. II. Title.

LB3012.P73 2007
371.5—dc22

2007000005

Contents

Chapter

Part Two:
Judicious Discipline in the Classroom—
Lesson Plans and Activities
for Building Democratic Classroom Communities

Chapter

Part Three:
Building Judicious Communities

Dedication

This book is dedicated to all the fine teachers and education students who have taught me so much about the needs of young people in our public schools. I appreciate their insight, celebrate their creativity, and am grateful that I can call them my colleagues.

This book is also dedicated to every K-12 student in every classroom. It is my deepest wish that the educators who touch their lives will effectively and equitably address all of their needs, abilities, and ambitions.

—*Barbara Landau*

Foreword

Forrest Gathercoal

The life of a writer is often a lonely one, due to the nature of the art and the absence of those with whom ideas might be shared. I feel very fortunate, however, that during much of the development of *Judicious Discipline* I had the opportunity to work with Barbara Landau who so ably edited the first edition. After her initial work on my book, she branched out and created a supplement for *Judicious Discipline* that would reflect the work teachers, administrators, and others have done to implement and fully integrate this classroom management framework based on rights and responsibilities.

Now on the faculty of the College of Education at the University of Hawaii, Barbara has continued to research effective strategies for implementing these concepts in classrooms and to work closely with many teachers and administrators practicing *Judicious Discipline* in their schools and classrooms. She has integrated the model's concepts with cooperative learning strategies as well as the classroom management methods of Rudolph Dreikurs, William Glasser, and others who advocate a democratic, student-centered approach to discipline.

It is with great enthusiasm that I recommend *Practicing Judicious Discipline*, now in its fourth edition. Barbara Landau has the ability to translate the raw material of principles into a meaningful and workable tool for classroom teachers. It is my hope that the ideas and lesson plans in this book will help educators establish and maintain a democratic environment in schools and classrooms. Only empowered educators are able to empower students with rights and responsibilities necessary to truly value learning from and interacting with others.

Editor's Foreword

Barbara Landau

Aloha! As Forrest Gathercoal says in his Foreword, I am now at the University of Hawaii, Manoa. I think it is important to share with you, the reader, that the problems with education are everywhere. Here in Hawaii some of our children live in poverty, some have special needs that are or are not identified, some come from other Pacific Island chains speaking primary languages other than English, and some come from cultures that are misunderstood or mistrusted by the majority cultures. The educational issues associated with being academically at-risk are not exotic or unique here, rather they are comparable to many of those on the United States mainland.

What I find here, just as I did when I lived up there, is that behaviorist management systems, all too common everywhere, work to the detriment of these students. When students drop out, which they do in increasingly large numbers, they say they are leaving because they feel misunderstood, they feel like outcasts, and they feel their teachers do not like them. Teachers do not have to "like" students, but we do have to treat them with respect and ensure their equal educational opportunities.

For all these reasons, I believe *Judicious Discipline* is more important now than ever. Democratic management is being lost in the drumbeat of No Child Left Behind's emphasis on test scores, drill, and practice. We cannot lose sight of the children we are serving. Their individual needs must be of paramount importance to all educators. When we ensure respect and equity in our schools and classrooms, we go a long way to bringing every child with us....and leaving no one behind.

Part One

Understanding the Basics of *Judicious Discipline*

Part One

Introduction

Barbara Landau

I have a picture on my bulletin board of the first class I ever taught, a Kindergarten class in a Midwestern inner-city school. My students were all African Americans and they came from nurturing homes or abusive homes, they experienced strong religious influences in their lives or no religious influences, they were desperately poor or were in lower-middle-class families. And within what appears on the surface to be a generic group of children, there were those who were learning disabled and those who were showing early signs of emotional disorder and children who were developmentally much younger than their peers and children who were showing early signs of true giftedness. We shared many values, yet the gulf between our life experiences sometimes seemed as large as the Grand Canyon.

I also have a picture of the last class I taught before moving on to pursue a doctorate. It was in a preschool in an upscale suburban neighborhood. My students were all Caucasian. The four-year-old children in that picture came from nurturing homes or abusive homes, they experienced strong religious influences in their lives or no religious influences, they were living in middle to upper-middle-class families. And within what appears on the surface to be a generic group of children, there were those who were learning disabled and those who were showing early signs of emotional disorder and children who were developmentally much younger than their peers and children who were showing early signs of true giftedness. We shared many values, yet the gulf between our life experiences sometimes seemed as large as the Grand Canyon.

The lesson I learned from teaching each class and from having taught both is that there exists no easy definition of what we mean when we say "diversity" or "special needs." It is too easy and too tempting to make quick decisions about the needs the students might or might not have based on their outward appearances. That sort of stereotyping poorly serves the needs of the children we teach and can result in educators failing to fulfill their professional responsibility towards helping every student experience success.

Curriculum, classroom management, and parent interactions would all be so much easier if our students were all alike and were all like the educators who teach them. What is particular to and challenging about the public school classroom is that our students may share no other common element, one to the other, than the proximity of their desks. Perhaps the homes they come from are near each other, perhaps not. Students may or may not share common values, creeds, cultures, or economic levels. They may very well be strangers to each other, and yet, even the youngest students will view their peers through the lens they have been given by their families and friends.

And we are their teachers, ready on any given day to begin the process of building a community spirit among these diverse learners. It is an easy mistake for us to label them generically and to make unfounded assumptions about them based on where they live, the color of their skin, and the number or gender of adults with whom they live. Equally dangerous is the temptation to think that if they look like us, they think like us. Students think and act in ways that are unique to them as products of their families, cultures, and their times. We can make no assumptions.

So I begin this Introduction with the lesson I learned in my years of classroom teaching, that diversity resides in all classrooms and within all children. Accepting that premise, the question becomes, how can teachers in today's public schools set about establishing a climate that will build a unified community out of all these various people?

As I have worked with *Judicious Discipline* over the past ten years, two elements have emerged that make this approach particularly well suited to serving the multiple interests of all students. First and foremost is the community-building language *Judicious Discipline* provides, language based on the balance between human rights and social responsibilities that supports an unbiased consistency for classroom decision-making. No matter how diverse the individual members of a community might be, when they come together in a *Judicious Discipline* classroom and use the language of rights and responsibilities for decision making, they learn to share common understandings and values that sustain our larger society as well as their own classroom communities (Gathercoal, 2004).

The second element is the manner in which the language of *Judicious Discipline* levels the playing field for all participants. When the language for classroom decision-making is based on human rights and civic responsibilities, it is far more likely that students will experience equitable decisions to support their learning opportunities and peacefully resolve their behavior problems. The legal framework provides a basis for viewing all classroom decisions from the perspective of what will best serve the needs of everyone. Assessment, learning tasks, emotional outbursts, and whatever else an average day includes; every issue can be approached through the use of a language that views all students as citizens in a free society with the incumbent responsibilities for maintaining the common welfare. *Judicious Discipline* is basically a synthesis of democratic principles, sound educational practice, and ethics that, put together, helps educators focus their teaching strategies on motivation, encouragement, and building positive self-concepts in every student.

A Quick Overview

Judicious Discipline teaches individual rights and how those rights are always being balanced against the compelling state interests that protect our society's need for a safe, healthy, and undisrupted environment. Teachers using *Judicious Discipline* in their classrooms begin by introducing students to their rights of freedom, justice, and equality. This is followed by an explanation of when those rights can and should be limited. If a teacher, administrator, or staff member is able to demonstrate that the actions of students threaten the health and safety, property, and/ or educational purpose of the school, then students would need some redirection, additional information and possibly some restrictions placed upon their freedoms.

Judicious Discipline focuses on an educator's professional responsibility to work with and teach every student, pointing out that learning self-discipline can and should be taught along with math, science, and social studies. One tool for helping students learn to correct their behavior problems and make good decisions about their actions might be a consequence. But rather than creating an arbitrary set of consequences that apply to any number of inappropriate behaviors, *Judicious Discipline* advocates approaching discipline problems as teachable moments. What does the student need to learn in order to avoid repeating the inappropriate behavior next time? What information does the teacher need to best help every student recover and go on to experiencing success? A number of options are possible from a conference to a written contract. A consequence may be useful but it should not be the first response to a problem and it must not be the only response.

Certainly there are other discipline models that subscribe to democratic practices. *Judicious Discipline* represents a unique addition to this body of work because it specifically sets out the legal framework for the decision-making process rather than leaving to chance an understanding of human rights and social responsibilities.

The intent of *Judicious Discipline* is not that it replaces other discipline models, but that it is used in conjunction with other student-centered approaches. It provides teachers and administrators with an equitable framework for making school and classroom decisions as they set about building learning environments that function to benefit everyone.

For *Judicious Discipline* to be effectively employed at a variety of educational levels in every demographic setting it must be viewed from a global perspective. To approach the concepts of rights and responsibilities from a "how do we use this to control kids" point of view is to severely limit the possibilities of what might occur in an educational environment that teaches individuals how to assume social responsibilities. The essence of social justice in classrooms is the appreciation of each student as a human being with diverse needs and abilities. While some students are more difficult to reach than others, *Judicious Discipline* firmly maintains that professional educators must never give up trying. Success may not always accompany our efforts, nevertheless professional ethics dictate the need to support and encourage even the most troubled young person.

How This Book Can Help

Creating a classroom environment that will provide equitable learning opportunities for all students requires careful thought and reflection. Information needs to be taught, expectations established, rights and responsibilities discussed. Deciding how a classroom will operate, what strategies will be used, and the role students will play in the process are just a few of the major decisions to be made by teachers as they structure their school year.

This book, as a supplement to Forrest Gathercoal's *Judicious Discipline,* is designed to give educators practical ideas for lesson plans, advice from educators who use *Judicious Discipline,* and a compendium of strategies designed to assist in the creation of a school-wide democratic learning environment that will serve the needs of all students.

This book offers its readers a variety of articles addressing the broadest range of diverse needs and interests present in any classroom. In addition, the reader is also provided with lesson plans, activities and other practical resources for successfully implementing the *Judicious Discipline* framework.

Conclusion

In the final analysis, *Judicious Discipline* is a framework for ensuring the permanent value of all students in all classrooms and, at the same time, promoting heightened levels of professionalism for educators. *Judicious Discipline* helps teachers establish equitable classrooms with consistent and careful regard for the needs each student brings to the classroom. Curriculum design, assessment strategies, classroom meetings, and classroom expectations do not turn a blind eye to the diverse needs of students; rather, *Judicious Discipline* helps teachers thoughtfully scrutinize those present in the classroom in order to ensure that their needs are being met.

Reference

Gathercoal, F. (2004). *Judicious discipline*, Fourth Edition. San Francisco: Caddo Gap Press.

Judicious Discipline and Neuroscience:
Constructing a Neurological Rationale for Democracy in the Classroom

Paul Gathercoal

Specific strategies for school discipline and classroom management based on models of behavior modification have become increasingly popular in American schools (Hill, 1990). As a result, most of our teachers and administrators have learned to mete out rewards and punishment in a systematic and ad-hoc fashion in hopes of controlling America's youth by reinforcing desirable behavior and discouraging unwanted behavior (McEwan, 1990). For many students, punishment or behaving out of fear of "getting caught" is the only model of discipline they experience throughout their formal schooling. And models of discipline which are based on fear and coercion operate only at the lowest levels of ethical reasoning on any taxonomy of moral development.

It is not surprising then that the reaction from America's youth to these behavioral models of discipline has not been favorable. When asked, students who attended schools where behavioral models of discipline were in force often tell me that they and their classmates felt "powerless." Possibly it is this feeling of powerlessness that has contributed to the large number of students "at risk" in American schools (Sarason, 1990). Behavioral models of school discipline have done little to instill a sense of responsible behavior in students and change is needed.

William Glasser (1985) echoes this call for change when he

9

says educators must "give up" coercion and stimulus/response techniques in schools. He states there are five genetically determined intrinsic motivators or "basic needs" that will sustain the potential for teaching and learning: survival, freedom, love and belonging, power, and fun. And these "basic needs" are the epistemological "heart and soul" of cognitive models for school discipline.

Educators who decide to move away from behavioral models of school discipline to cognitive models like *Judicious Discipline* must implement such dramatic change incrementally over a period of time (Gathercoal, 1991). These things take time because there is no context for understanding or visualizing cognitive discipline practices when the only model students, teachers, and parents/caregivers have known is a coercive behavioral model.

To exemplify this notion, I am reminded of one of my second-grade students who wrote and submitted an article for final editing and inclusion in our first class newsletter that was to be sent home to parents/caregivers. In the article, the student expressed concern that there was a lot of fighting going on in our classroom and that I was doing nothing about it. It was early in the year, after we had addressed the principles of *Judicious Discipline* and established our class expectations, but had yet to talk about consequences. As a result, my way of dealing with the fighting was seen, at least by this student, as doing nothing about it. This was probably because the strategies I used were transparent to students who were not involved. This particular student saw no names on the board, heard no warnings being issued, and observed no public ridicule being meted out. There were, however, quiet talks that resulted in negotiated and commensurate consequences assigned to the offending behavior. All of this remained confidential and so was not obvious to others until we talked about appropriate consequences as a class. It was some time later that the concerned student approached me and requested that I not publish the article "about the fighting in our class." Incremental changes based on present practice and extending toward future practice helped to provide context for change and make the new disciplinary practices apparent instead of transparent.

In order to help students and ourselves prepare for dramatic change we must construct a framework for this process. We can do this by understanding that it takes *time* to educate our community of students, fellow educators, and parents/caregivers, and we need to provide understandable metaphors for change (Langer, 1989; Lipsitt, 1990; Restak, 1988; Squire, 1987). These metaphors connect the new ideas embedded in *Judicious Discipline* to what are currently accepted practices.

Time is necessary because the fabric or context for change cannot be constructed overnight. We need "consolidation time" (Kandel, 1994). "Consolidation time" is the time after a learning experience when the brain physically changes, neurologically, biochemically, and genetically, in order to store in long-term memory that which was learned. If "consolidation time" is interrupted, the learning will not be transferred from working memory to long-term memory, and all that was learned will fade away (Kandel, 1994). The message we learn from this is that we need to provide time for our students to consolidate their learning and we need to link what is being learned to the known (Edleman, 1987; Grossberg, 1980; Ornstein & Thompson, 1984). Incremental implementation of *Judicious Discipline*, over a period of time that metaphorically links the new to the old, helps weave this fabric of neurons, biochemicals, and genes that prepare students for teaching and learning in the democratic classroom. To better understand this need for *incremental implementation*, time, and *neuronal, biochemical, and genetic adaptation in the brain*, let us consider the biological link between cognition (thought) and behavior (action).

All Learning Is Biological

Consider that the brain's shape and biochemical makeup is physically affected by an individual's experience and metaphorical imagination, and this affect is fueled by memory and perception (Kandel, Schwartz, & Jessell, 1991; Levinthal, 1990; Restak, 1988; Squire, 1987). Simply put, the brain is "plastic." It is a combination of our experience and metaphorical imaginings that help to construct new neurological and biochemical connections—a fabric for change. As a result, the brain continually adapts to new input and redefines appropriate behavior, and this is reflected in our ever-changing ideas, beliefs, attitudes, and values. We physically construct neuronal circuits with balanced states of biochemical and electrical activity and these become our conceptual maps of social reality and our cultural ways of knowing; these are our schemata.

Schemata are neurologically, biochemically, and genetically constructed. They are fabricated in a language framework of social origins. Language is the DNA of schema. It is from language that all the building blocks emerge that can be used to design a way of knowing. By configuring the language into meaningful symbols and communicating these symbols to significant others, mental templates of culture and tradition are formed and these become the reference points for conceptual mapping and schema development and they act as our political guidance systems.

The mental templates individuals construct encode previous ways of understanding. And the previous ways of understanding are embedded in metaphors. As the metaphors of understanding are transmitted from individual to individual, the language that is used to develop schema may change the metaphors of understanding and thus alter the mental templates of culture and tradition. In this way language is intertwined with schema development. The language can both facilitate and hide interests. As a result, there is great power invested in those who control the language and the channels of transmission used to construct schema.

Schema are developed through a holistic interplay between the cognitive, affective, and psycho-motor domains. Emotion, thought, and the physical body are all intrinsically linked, one affecting the other in a cascade of biochemical, neurological, and genetic activity (Damasio, 1994; Sylwester, 1995; Goeman, 1995). In his book, *Descartes' Error*, Antonio R. Damasio (1994) cites evidence to support the existence of a "somatic marker system" (somatic meaning "body") or an acquired "gut feeling" that people use for making decisions about social living. This "gut feeling" is made up from our emotional response to a situation or thing and our body awareness, and it is absolutely essential for successful social living and pro-social decision-making. Damasio suggests that somatic markers or "gut feelings" are acquired emotional overtones that mediate rational thought processes. These "gut feelings" are linked to various events in our lives, whether real or imagined, and they are metaphorically transferred to new situations. In this way, they assist cognitive processing by providing a tacit emotional and concomitant body response when attending to the perceived consequences of a planned actions. For example, we can experience negative "gut feelings" when contemplating decisions and actions that run a risk to our own health and safety, e.g., running in a crowded hallway may not be the best way to move to the next class, or going skydiving without proper instruction is probably not the best choice for recreational activity; and we can experience positive "gut feelings" that are based on notions of delayed gratifications, e.g., doing "hard work" in math class will benefit me and others in the long run, or cleaning up my bedroom will prevent health and safety risks in the future.

Damasio found that some people are physically unable to develop or use a somatic marker system. He notes that these people are the exceptions and that they are not "normal." For example, some trauma patients he was working with had brain damage to the left anterior frontal lobe, and they had lost the ability to acquire or use previously acquired somatic markers, or "gut feelings." He also found that psychopaths and sociopaths do not seem to experience the full range of feelings of guilt or remorse for their antisocial actions, and that all of these people who are not "normal" tend to live their lives as a disaster, making poor life decisions with disastrous effects for themselves and the people around them.

This is how we learn and know how to behave. We change biologically and act accordingly (Kandel, et. al., 1991; Levinthal, 1990; Ornstein & Thompson, 1984). Given this close association between experience and imagination, cognition and behavior, it is logical to think that if an individual only experiences coercive, stimulus/response classroom management practices, s/he will probably learn to operate at the lowest levels of moral development. S/he will constantly ask, "What's in it for me?," because that is the way s/he will be "wired" to respond. For students who have been subjected to coercive/behavioral models of school discipline for most of their lives, the proposition of being held accountable or responsible for their own learning and behavior can be a shock to their neuronal circuits. After years of fine tuning neuronal circuits which activate behavior designed to avoid possible punishment and seek probable rewards, it may be difficult for students to come to terms with the rigors of being self-disciplined, responsible citizens in a democratic classroom. Students will need to be taught about their democratic rights and responsibilities and given the *time* and opportunities to experience and imagine so they can *physically* change their neuronal connections and biochemical activity in order to accommodate the new experience of living and learning in a democratic environment.

Judicious Discipline provides educators with opportunities to challenge their students' neuronal circuits by offering students "neurological time" to consider alternatives. Imagine the opportunities for teaching and learning when students with problems are requested by the educator to, "Tell me about it," instead of confronted with "who dunit?" Rather than activating what is known as a stereotypical response circuit, i.e. "It wasn't me!," students are given an opportunity to take "neurological time" and access other ideas via alternative neuronal circuits. They enjoy an opportunity to tell the educator about their problem. In so doing, they access neuronal circuits that recall perceptions, offer explanations, make predictions, and suggest possible choices. These are the higher level thinking processes that educators hope to tap into during every lesson.

It follows that educators who practice *Judicious Discipline* will give their students repeated opportunities for practicing higher level thinking. And as a result, it is likely that "It wasn't me!" will disappear from students' repertoire of stereotypical responses. Concomitantly, they will learn to favor more self-reflecting responses which indicate an ownership of behavior and a responsibility for their actions.

The Endorphin Connection

Endorphins (*Endo*genous Mo*rphines*) are very powerful peptides, composed of small chains of amino acids. They act as neurotransmitters (the basic unit of action in the brain). When released in the brain, they attach themselves to receptors on specific brain cells or neurons. Endorphins are very important. Our bodies physically need them. In fact, we are addicted to endorphin activity. If we do not synthesize, release, and bind endorphins to specific brain cells we will go through a "withdrawal" similar to that of a heroin addict (Beck & Beck, 1987; Levinthal, 1988).

Endorphins are involved in maintaining health; mediating emotions, pain, and stress; and providing intrinsic reward (Kehoe, 1988). They perform these functions by relieving pain and/or inducing feelings of pleasure. It is the endorphin link with intrinsic reward that is most fascinating and adds support to Glasser's (1985) notion that there are five genetically determined intrinsic motivators. In fact, all five of Glasser's "basic needs" can be genetically explained, at least in part, as being mediated by endorphin activity in the brain.

Consider that individuals can be predisposed to certain behaviors that are mediated by endorphin activity; that is, an individual may get a "good feeling" because s/he acts a certain way in a social situation. Inappropriate behaviors in school, when interpreted in this light, can then be viewed as behaviors that are endorphin activating for one student but infringing on the rights and interests of the rest of the class. Teachers responding to such inappropriate behavior with coercive, stimulus/response discipline strategies apparently believe they can provide students with extrinsic rewards that will exceed the intrinsic rewards of endorphin activity students probably feel when they display the inappropriate behavior.

The problem with this approach is that the offending behavior still acts as endorphin-activating experiences and the student has acquired new ways of seeking "love and belonging," "power," "freedom," "fun," and even "survival" that are all dependent upon the school providing tangible reinforcers. In other words, the student never owns the problem, but reaps even more benefits as a result of it and always at the expense of others. The student who is put on a behavior modification program to control "attention getting" outbursts in class is still in a power struggle with authority. S/he is still intent upon seeking power through acquiring some form of tangible reward—whether it be positive comments from the teacher or "beans-in-a-jar"—and if the rewards for conforming to the teacher's expectations are not great enough, s/he need only resort to the offensive behavior once more to assert power over the class environment.

Only when the desired behavior is intrinsically rewarding to the student will s/he ultimately change. *Judicious Discipline* can assist with this transition by helping misbehaving students imagine ways they can meet their "physical needs" for socially stimulated endorphin activity by behaving in institutionally okay ways and helping to provide a neurological context for change at the same time.

The Effect of Media Messages on Behavior

Another effect of endorphin activity may be closely linked to modeling via the media and their messages. Students who continually rely on commercial media messages for role models and use them as guides for mentally rehearsing successful social behaviors are probably glorifying behaviors that are antithetical to acceptable, ethical behavior in schools. Students who emulate their favorite star's mannerisms and stereotyped behaviors may expect violence and coercion to solve problems, think that any social problem can be completely solved within a short period of time, and that sex role stereotypes are accurate reflections of our society and the expected norm.

Consider the majority of "007" films screened in cinemas around the world, re-run on commercial television, and rented on videotape. Male students may learn from the featured male role model that to be successful in love they need to act macho and aloof and treat women as mere objects. Female students may learn that they need to be slender, with "perfect" hair and teeth, and that they *are* mere objects for men's pleasure. While educators try very hard

16

to instill a sense of "it's okay to be you and me," the messages of the commercial media tend to compromise this premise in a very powerful way. And even those students with the strongest self-concept will pause a moment to compare their self-images with those images presented by the commercial media. *Judicious Discipline* gives students a sense of "permanent value" (Dreikurs, 1968) and provides opportunities for students to reflect upon the dichotomy of modal values exposed by schools and commercial media. Schools advocate modal values like honesty, caring, sharing, and cooperation and commercial media messages often advocate modal values like violence, competition, and egocentric behaviors. Teaching students about individual rights and responsibilities conveys the message that everyone has a right to feel physically and mentally safe and secure and that everyone has a responsibility to ensure that these feelings are extended throughout society. Students learn that they are important individuals, too, especially when the judicious educator takes time to listen to their side of the story, acts with professional courage, and negotiates appropriate consequences for breaches in rules. Implicitly, the educator is sending a powerful message about the importance of the individual.

This kind of behavior from educators is antithetical to the behavior generally displayed in commercial films and television. When modeling such alternative behaviors for students, the judicious educator is laying a context, a fabric of neurological connections, which helps prepare students for ideological change. Educators who model behavior based on democratic principles implicitly challenge their students to question the fantastic nature of super-hero behaviors and the "glitz" associated with dramatized films and commercial television programs.

Providing Context: A Role for *Judicious Discipline*

Individuals who need greater and greater endorphin activity to achieve a "good feeling" or who constantly activate specific, stereotypical neuronal circuitry in response to social and problem situations may become caught up in their own pleasure and be desensitized to the needs and desires of their living environment. This is when *Judicious Discipline* can provide a new context for understanding and assist individuals to realize that their rights are always balanced against the interests of the rest of society. Through education (involving experience and metaphorical imagination) we can affect student cognition, affection, and behavior by helping our students make new neuronal connections with concomitant balanced states of biochemical activity.

When educators use *Judicious Discipline*, the effect on all who are involved is to construct a neurological fabric for critical thinking and peaceful social living. However, the reality is that this effect will not be immediate; it will take time. Even though this effect will take some time, the benefits are well worth it in the long run. The good news is, the effect will probably be long lasting and transferable from social situation to social situation. Educators need to realize that *time* is an educational resource that we have available to us and we should expand time to accommodate and tap into the "basic needs" of our students (fun, power, freedom, love and belonging, and survival).

As educators we should realize that we affect our students by physically changing their genetic makeup through experience and metaphorical imagination, which affects their predisposition for cognition and behavior. Only cognitive models for school discipline, like that of *Judicious Discipline*, will effect such long lasting change in our students. Coercive, stimulus/response models will only effect change for specific situations; and unless accompanied by some intrinsic motivation, the learned behavior will not be transferred from problem situation to problem situation. It is cognitive models, like *Judicious Discipline*, that will help prepare our nation's students for living and learning in a democratic society.

References

Beck, D., & Beck, J. (1987). *The pleasure connection*. San Francisco: Synthesis Press.

Damasio, A. (1994) *Descartes' error*. New York: G.P. Putnam's Sons.

DeFleur, M.L., & Ball-Rokeach, S. (1990). *Theories of mass communication*, 5th Ed., White Plains, NY: Longman.

Dreikurs, R. (1968). *Psychology in the classroom: A manual for teachers*, 2nd Ed. New York: Harper & Row.

Edleman, G.M. (1987). *Neural darwinism: The theory of neuronal group selection*. New York: Basic Books.

Gardner, L. (1983). *Frames of mind: The theory of multiple intelligences*. New York: Basic Books.

Gathercoal, F. (2004). *Judicious discipline*, 4th Ed. San Francisco: Caddo Gap Press.

Gathercoal, P. (1990). Brain research and mediated experience: An interpretation of the implications for education. *The Clearing House*, 63(6), 271-273.

Gathercoal, P. (1991). A technology for policy implementation: Minimizing incongruity between ostensible policy and the policy at work. *Educational Technology*, 31(3), 47-50.

Gathercoal, P., & Quin, R. (1993). On interactive media and hidden agendas. *Quarterly Journal of Ideology*, 16(3&4), 77-84.

Glasser, W. (1986). *Control theory in the classroom*. New York: Harper & Row.

Goldstein, A. (1980). Thrills in response to music and other stimuli. *Physiological Psychology*, 8(1), 126-129.

Goleman, D. (1995). *Emotional intelligence*, New York: Bantam Books.

Grossberg, S. (1980). How does a brain build a cognitive code? *Physiological Review*, 87(1), 1-39.

Hill, D. (April, 1990). Order in the classroom. *Teacher*, 70-77.

Kandel, E.R., Schwartz, J.H., & Jessell, T. M. (1991). *Principles of neural science*, 3rd Ed. New York: Elsevier.

Kehoe, P. (1988). Opiods, behavior, and learning in mammalian development. In E.M. Blass (Ed.), *Handbook of behavioral neurobiology: Volume 9: Developmental psychobiology and behavioral ecology*, (pp. 309-346). New York: Plenum Press.

Lammers, J.H.C.M., van der Noordaa, J., Kruk, M.R., Meelis, W., & van der Poel, G.M. (1989). Interactions between simultaneously activated behavioral systems in the rat. *Behavioral Neuroscience*, 103(4), 784-789.

Langer, E.J. (1989). *Mindfulness*. Reading, MA: Addison-Wesley.

Levinthal, C.F. (1990). *Introduction to physiological psychology*. Englewood Cliffs, NJ: Prentice Hall.

Levinthal, C.F. (1988). *Messengers of paradise: Opiates and the brain*. New York: Anchor Press.

Levitt, R.A., Stilwell, D.J., & Evers, T.M. (1978). Brief communication: Morphine and shuttlebox self-stimulation in the rat: Tolerance studies. *Pharmacology Biochemistry & Behavior*, 9, 567-569.

Lipsitt, L.P. (1990). Learning processes in the human newborn. In A. Diamond (Ed.), *The development and neural bases of higher cognitive functions*. New York: The New York Academy of Sciences.

McEwan, B. (1990). Review: *Judicious Discipline. Democracy and Education*, 4(3), 37-40.

Ornstein, R., & Ehrlich, P. (1990). *New world new mind*. New York: Simon & Schuster.

Ornstein, R., & Thompson, R.F. (1984). *The amazing brain*. Boston, MA: Houghton Mifflin.

Restak, R.M. (July/August, 1992). See no evil: The neurological defense would blame violence on the damaged brain. *The Sciences*, 16-21.

Restak, R.M. (1988). *The mind*. New York: Bantam Books.

Sarason, S.B. (1990). *The predictable failure of educational reform*. San Francisco: Jossey-Bass.

South Australian Council for Children's Films and Television, Inc. (1986). *Kids and the scary world of video*. A Study of Video Viewing Among 1498 Primary School Children in South Australia, published by the Television Committee of the South Australian Council for Children's Films and Television, Incorporated.

Squire, L.R. (1987). *Memory and brain*. New York: Oxford University Press.

Media Literacy for Children and Youth:

An Assets and Acquisitions Approach

Donna Grace

Literacy has traditionally been associated with the written word. However, in today's media-saturated society, print literacy is no longer adequate. Children and youth are growing up "reading" a multitude of texts that include film, television, videos, DVDs, computer games, and Internet websites, in addition to books. Digital literacies play an increasingly large role in the everyday lives of students. Whether you like it or not, the media is here to stay. Given these facts, it is neither realistic to expect that we can shield children from the media, nor wise to think that we should. As David Buckingham has stated, the media are the major contemporary means of cultural expression and communication today. The goal is to enable youth "to make informed decisions on their own behalf" as members of society (2003, p.13). Rather than a form of protection, media education needs to be seen as a form of preparation for life. As asserted by Richard Riley, former U.S. Secretary of Education, "Our young people need to be educated to the highest standard in this new information age, and surely this includes a clear awareness of how the media influences, shapes, and defines their lives" (in Pack, 2002, p.10).

If we are to have an informed and critical future citizenry, today's youth must learn to 'read' and interpret visual images, reflect on their use of the media, and develop understandings

21

about media construction and conventions. Students need to become aware of how media texts convey particular messages, values, and points of view, and how people are represented and positioned in terms of race, ethnicity, class, gender, age, body type and body-ableness, among other things. This is where media literacy comes in. As part of a wider move towards democratization in the classroom, media education seeks to develop a critical autonomy in students by enabling them to make informed judgments about the media texts that they engage with as both consumers and producers of media (Buckingham, 2003).

Media literacy is commonly defined as the ability to analyze, evaluate, and produce media for specific outcomes. It is mandated in the curriculum in Canada, Australia, and Great Britain, and media education has appeared increasingly in America's classrooms in recent years. The need for media literacy is presented in national as well as state standards. As stated in the National Health Education Standards, "Students will analyze the influence of culture, media, technology, and other factors on health" (Joint Commission on the National Health Standards, 1995). The National Standards for the English Language Arts also call for students to "apply knowledge of language structure, language conventions, media techniques, figurative language, and genre to create, critique, and discuss print and nonprint text" (IRA & NCTE, 1996).

Traditionally, media education has been structured around a deficit model that portrays the media as harmful, kids as passive and helpless victims, and media literacy as the key to helping students to see the error of their ways. A more effective approach to take is an assets and acquisition model. Here, teachers view the knowledge students have about the media as a foundation for helping them to acquire new skills and abilities. Many media educators have long-advocated for a more student-centered and strengths-based model of media education and research (Buckingham, 1990, 2003; Desmond, 1997; Goodman, 2003; Tobin, 2000; Tyner, 1998). Utilizing this approach, educators recognize young people's experience with and knowledge of the media and build upon it in ways that are educationally sound. As

22

stated by Tyner (1998), such a model "assumes that mass media and popular culture content can work as a benefit to literacy instead of as a social deficit" (7). There is a long-standing body of research to support this perspective. Susan Newman (1988) reported that a modest amount of television viewing appeared to be positively related to young children's reading scores. Braggs (2002) and Newman (1997) both found that the skills and information that children and youth acquire from their experiences with the media, such as knowledge about genre, plot, character development, setting, and narrative structure, transfer directly to print literacy. In another study Rakes (1999) found evidence to suggest that short term working memory can be increased by presenting the same information in different media forms. Greenfield's research (1984) demonstrates that playing video and computer games enhances cognitive development and motor skills.

In addition to using students' knowledge about the media to bridge to more traditional notions of literacy, it also serves as a foundation for acquiring *new* knowledge and abilities. These new areas of learning include technology, the production process, key concepts of the media, and the analytical skills needed to help students become more informed critical viewers *and* creators of the media. We need keep in mind that the youth today are the media makers of tomorrow!

Following some preliminary decoding/recoding media activities, one of the most effective ways to develop media literacy in students is through the production process. Media projects can be incorporated into any content area, and might take the form of a school newspaper, class comic book, poetry video, closed-circuit TV news show, public service announcement, short film, or video documentary, among other things. In such projects, students gain an understanding of the purpose, structure, and style of different media genres. Critical viewing skills are developed in ways that emerge naturally and authentically from the production process. As students construct criteria to evaluate the media they create, they acquire the interest and ability to transfer these skills to the media they view. Providing students with the opportunity to have ownership over this process is much more effective than teacher lectures on the motives and manipulations of the media, or time spent deconstructing students' out-of-school media pleasures. Through hands-on, active learning, students construct knowledge about the key concepts of media literacy (Leveranz & Tyner, 1993):

Industry: industrial/commercial aspects; sources of finance; power & profit motives.

Genre: different types of media texts; different features and expectations.

Technology: tools and materials needed to produce media texts.

Language: words, images, music, camera shots & angles; how and why they are used.

Audience: targeted audience; ways in which they are constructed; potential media effects.

Representation: stereotyping; bias; values; point of view.

As students are enabled to become producers, rather than merely consumers of the media, they are provided with opportunities to mediate, rework, and in some cases resist some of the messages of the media (Grace & Tobin, 2002). In addition, the production process broadens career awareness, and breaks down some gender boundaries, particularly for girls, as they learn new technologies and experiment with roles in video productions that are typically coded as masculine (Grace, 2003).

Incorporating the goals of *Judicious Discipline*, the asset and acquisition model of media education contributes to a more democratic learning environment in at least four important ways. First, the home-school disconnect is lessened by acknowledging and validating the students' everyday interests and experiences with the media. Typically, the shared cultural knowledge that youth possess about the media is either devalued in school or excluded from the classroom completely. Second, media education contributes to a more informed and critical citizenry by developing the skills that will allow children and youth to analyze the influence and impact of the media on themselves and on society (Buckingham, 2003, p. 5). In Paul Gathercoals's discussion of *Judicious Discipline* in this book (see pages 9-20), he underscores the need for students to be provided with opportunities to reflect on the messages conveyed through the media, and to consider whether they promote pro-social or anti-social values and behaviors. Third, while producing their own media, students are actively engaged in projects that are motivating, meaningful and relevant to their lives. In the process, collaborative and problem-solving skills are enhanced while respect for others is fostered. Students typically alienated from their schooling may also find an entry way to engaging with school curriculum. Fourth, through the production process, students are able to give voice to their own interests, issues, concerns and pleasures. A student-produced comic book or a parody of an advertisement, for instance, can provide opportunities for humor while learning about the codes and conventions of these genres. A classroom newspaper, a public service announcement, or a video documentary project can empower students to research issues in their school and community and to become advocates for change.

References

Bragg, S. (2002). Wrestling in woolly gloves: Not just being critically media literate. *Journal of Popular Film and Television, 30* (1), 42-52.

Buckingham, D. (1990). *Watching media learning: Making sense of media education*. New York: Falmer Press.

Buckingham, D. (2003). *Media education: Literacy, learning and contemporary culture*. Cambridge, UK: Polity Press.

Christensen, L. (1994). Unlearning the myths that bind us: Critiquing fairy tales and films. In *Rethinking our classrooms: Teaching for equity and justice*. Milwaukee, WI: Rethinking Schools.

Desmond, R. (1997). TV Viewing, Reading and Media Literacy. In Flood, Heath, & Lapp, *Handbook of research on teaching literacy through the communicative and visual arts*, (pp. 23-30). Mahwah, NJ: Lawrence Erlbaum Associates.

Goodman, S. (2003). *Teaching youth media: A critical guide to literacy, video production, and social change*. New York: Teachers College

Press.

Grace, D. (2003). Gender, power and pleasure: Integrating student video production into the elementary curriculum. *Curriculum Perspectives, 23* (1), 21-27.

Grace, D., & Tobin, J. (2002). Pleasure, creativity, and the carnivalesque in children's video production. In L. Bresler & C. M. Thompson (Eds.), *The arts in children's lives: Context, culture, and curriculum*. Boston: Kluwer Academic Publishers.

Greenfield, P. (1984). *Mind and media: The effects of television, video games, and computers*. Cambridge, MA: Harvard University Press.

International Reading Association & National Council of Teachers of English. (1996). *Standards for the English language arts*. Newark, DE: International Reading Association.

Joint commission on National Health Education Standards. (1995). *National health education standards: Achieving health literacy*. Atlanta, GA: American Cancer Society.

Leveranz, D., & Tyner, K. (1993). Inquiring minds want to know: What is media literacy? *The Independent*, Aug./Sept., 21-19.

Newman, S. (1997). Television as a Learning Environment: A theory of synergy. In Flood, Heath, & Lapp, *Handbook of research on teaching literacy through the communicative and visual arts*, (pp. 15-22). Mahwah, NJ: Lawrence Erlbaum Associates.

Newman, S. (1998). The displacement effect: Assessing the relation between television viewing and reading performance. *Reading Research Quarterly, 23*, 414-440.

Ohta, R. (2006). A.B.C. Prunes, U.F.O. News, and Politicks: Parody in media literacy education. *Educational Perspectives, 38*(2), 12-16, www.hawaii.edu/edper/

Pack, T. (2002). Media literacy: educational organizations advocate enlightened media consumption. *Link-Up, 19*(3), 10.

Rakes, G. (1999). Literacy in a multimedia age. *Tech Trends, 43*(4), 14-18.

Tobin, J. (2000). *"Good guys don't wear hats:" Children's talk about the media*. New York: Teachers College Press.

Tyner, K. (1998). *Literacy in a digital world*. Mahwah, NJ: Lawrence Erlbaum Associates.

A Safe and Nurturing Classroom Environment Promotes the Mental and Emotional Well-Being of Students:
Recognizing Unique Qualities in Everyone

A. Ku'ulei Serna

Big Idea: A safe and nurturing classroom environment can be used to facilitate an individual's mental and emotional wellbeing. Mentally healthy children ... enjoy a positive quality of life and function well at home, school, and in their communities (Telljohann, S.K., Symons, C. W., & Pateman, B., 2006, p.119). The mental and emotional health of students can be key to their academic success. Students who feel comfortable, safe, challenged, cared for, and connected to school are more likely to succeed academically and have increased chances of avoiding participation in risk behaviors of violence and substance abuse (Telljohann, S.K., Symons, C. W., & Pateman, B., 2006).

When building a safe classroom environment, educators should pay close attention to actively promoting mental and emotional health. Creating opportunities within the curriculum for students to learn and maintain health-enhancing behaviors would definitely promote the practice of mental and emotional wellbeing. Teachers can promote mentally and emotionally healthy behavior outcomes for students by teaching them to:

· Express feelings in a healthy way.

· Engage in activities that are mentally and emotionally healthy.

27

· Prevent and/or manage internal conflict and stress in healthy ways.

· Use self-control and impulse control strategies to promote health.

· Seek help for troublesome feelings.

· Be empathetic toward others.

· Carry out personal responsibilities.

· Establish and maintain healthy relationships.
(Telljohann, S.K., Symons, C. W., & Pateman, B., 2006).

This list can help teachers create lessons or plan activities that encourage students to practice desired healthy behaviors concerning mental and emotional health.

Having students engage in activities that are mentally and emotionally healthy may include activities that build self-esteem. Reynold Bean (1992) states that research has indicated there are four conditions that make up a child's high self-esteem. They are:

(1) Sense of Being Connected: Students must feel that they are a part of or related to specific people, places or things, identify with a group, feel connected to a past or heritage, have a sense of ownership, feel good about the things they feel a part of, and know that the people or things they feel connected to are thought well of by others.

(2) Sense of Uniqueness: Students must know what is special about themselves, are able to enjoy being different, feel they are affirmed for what they are as opposed to judged for they are not, feel they respect self, know that other people think they are special feel creative and imaginative and have opportunities to safely express that.

(3) Sense of Power: Students feel that they are in charge of their own lives, believe that they can do what they set out to accomplish, feel others can't make them do things they really don't want to do, know they're not going to

lose control of themselves under pressure, and know they can get what they need to do what they have to do.

(4) Sense of Models: Students must know is when people are worthy of being emulated, feel confident they can tell right from wrong, have consistent values and beliefs that guide and direct their actions in different situations, feel a sense of purpose and know where they are headed, are able to make sense of what's going on in their lives, know the standards being used to judge them and have a sense of their own standards, a sense of order enabling them to organize their environment in order to accomplish tasks.

Teachers can use these basic principals of self-esteem to think about the way they behave and plan classroom activities to engage students in practicing desired health behavior regarding self-esteem. For example, it is the teacher's responsibility to create a safe and inclusive classroom environment to help students develop a sense of being connected (Telljohann, S., Symons, C., & Pateman, B., 2004).

Teachers should also think of ways to bring out uniqueness and gifts of students, as well as, incorporate interests of students in activities and/or curriculum to help develop a sense of uniqueness. To help students develop a sense of power, teachers can provide students with the skills necessary to accomplish tasks that are challenging that when finished, students feel satisfied about their success. Finally, with high standards and organization as a priority, teachers can help students develop a sense of models. It is also important that teachers demonstrate fairness and consistency (Telljohann, S., Symons, C., & Pateman, B., 2004). This provides a classroom environment that will enable students to accomplish goals.

References

Bean, R. (1992). *The four conditions of self-esteem: a new approach for elementary and middle schools,* 2nd Ed. Santa Cruz, CA: ETR Associates.

Parr, T. (2001). *It's okay to be different.* New York: Little, Brown &

Company.

Telljohann, S., Symons, C., & Pateman, B. (2004). *Health education: Elementary and middle school applications*, 4th Ed. Dubuque, IA: McGraw Hill.

Telljohann, S.K., Symons, C. W., & Pateman, B. (2006). *Health education: Elementary and middle school applications*, 5th Ed. New York: McGraw-Hill.

Empowering Teachers, Children, and Youth through the Visual Arts

Jennifer Herring

Art is a vital component in the transmission of knowledge, skills, and culture throughout our world. Understanding how the arts communicate and how the arts shape and reflect culture unlocks a language about who we are, what we think, and how we feel; and it can open our hearts and minds to the experience of others. The focus of this chapter is to encourage you to explore the visual arts alongside your students, valuing each other as artists, appreciating the role of the arts in our lives, building on our shared experiences in the arts to create new images to share with each other, and responding to what we are experiencing.

Engaging in the Arts in a Democratic Classroom

It is through the arts and the imagination that students can create meaning in the present and construct a vision for their future. Exploring the imagination, creative solutions, and various points of view is an avenue for an appreciation for those that are different from us. It is the imaginings of those that came before us that have placed us where we are now. Our imaginations help us conceptualize our universe, empathize with others, and realize our potential.

Empowering teachers, children, and youth through the arts

requires creating a democratic classroom where all voices are sought out, encouraged, and affirmed; where risk-taking is valued; where we meet each other as individuals in a shared space; where we support each others' failures and successes; and where we communicate our experiences and dreams.

Creating a Classroom Environment that Embraces the Arts and Each Other

Creating a sense of aesthetics in the classroom has the capacity to transform the learning environment into a space that is welcoming, engaging, relaxing, and inspiring. The aesthetics of the classroom can have an impact on the levels of engagement in learning and on the attitudes of the teachers and the students who work there. One of the most inviting classrooms experienced is a space where the students take care of the elements in the room that make it an interesting and engaging place to "live."

Insuring emotional security within a classroom is essential for creating a space that is aesthetically pleasing to the ear and the heart, where voices show care and concern for each other. Creating an environment where all responses are accepted and valued is evoked from constructing great questions that make this possible. Modeling a kind tone of voice and consistent validation encourages active participation in discussions. Knowing that each student is a unique individual with something to offer to the group is modeled in wanting to find our what our students already know, are able to do and care about.

Finding Out What Students Know, Are Able To Do, and Care about in the Arts

A highly effective process to experience along with your students is outlined in the thematic unit that appears in Part Two of this book. The unit begins with and focuses on the essential question, "Who am I as an artist and how are the arts a part of my life?" I like to model using inclusive language when talking with our students about the experiences included in the unit. The unit

32

also serves to build a strong sense of community in our democratic classroom where we value each other and share different ways to communicate about our experiences in the world around us. I want to encourage the teacher to start by engaging in the activities in the unit yourself, so you can share your presentation with the students in the same way you want the students to share with each other. Visual arts in the lives of students may include doodling, sketching, ceramics, photography, selecting fabric designs for our clothing or home, flower arranging, and food presentation. Other ways that the arts are a part of one's life may include watching movies, looking at magazines, selecting something to purchase, or describing a favorite tree or park. These are just a few possible examples and many times teachers or students may choose to focus on the ways in which they are a performing artist, such as a dancer, a musician, a singer, or an actor. Or explore how the performing arts are a part of our daily lives. As a facilitator of this discussion, I like to accept all of these possibilities and may even engage in exploring an aesthetic dilemma that asks the question, "What is art?" to see what students are thinking.

Asking, "What is Art?"

The opportunities to build on the question "What is art?" are endless and some exploration may include discussions about the value of art and what art students value most. We could even ask if the art we make in our classroom is as important as the artwork that is found in museum collections? And we can go further to explore who determines the value of a work of art? These questions open up thinking that can be transferred to other disciplines to examine critically the points of view from which literature and history is recorded and retold and how the point of view changes the essence of the story. Another opportunity to value different perspectives is created. Exploring the arts and becoming knowledgeable in the arts is a process that is important to share alongside your students in the safe risk-taking environment created for both teacher and the student to learn together.

Developing Open-Ended Questions

Another highly effective strategy is to ask your students to look at a finished work of art and try to define the aspects of the work that contribute to its success. Recording what students say helps in developing a student-created rubric that can be used to guide the production of quality products through the art process while developing skills in looking at art and articulating what is observed and experienced. Questions may focus on the story the piece tells, the process the artist used, the elements and principles of art and design, the feelings the work conveys, or curriculum connections that connect the subject matter of the work to content in the curriculum (Cornett, 2004).

Teaming with an Artist in Your Community

Another way to become more knowledgeable in the visual arts is to invite a professional or practicing artist from your community to come into your class to collaborate with you to develop experiences for you and your students. The artist can share her/his work with you and your students and you can plan together how to engage in an authentic experience that builds on the strengths of the visiting artist to work with the students in creating their own works of art. The artist will be learning from the teacher while the teacher will be learning from the artist through experiencing the process alongside the students. In essence, the practicing artist can tell you who they are as an artist and how the arts are a part of their lives. The practicing artist can also share with you and your students the artwork and the artists that influenced their work and reveal what they are trying to communicate through their own work. Most importantly the artist can engage you and your students in developing specific skills in using media and techniques in your own work.

Assessing Learning through Experiences in the Arts

The National Assessment of Educational Progress (NAEP) conducts periodic assessment on student achievement. In 1997,

NAEP administered the first national assessment that focused on the National Standards in the Fine Arts that include dance, music, theatre, and the visual arts (Persky, Snadene, & Askew, 1998). NAEP developed and implemented the arts content framework that included creating, performing and responding as the three art processes that should be included in arts assessment as follows:

Creating refers to expressing ideas and feelings in the form of an original work of art, for example, a dance, a piece of music, a dramatic improvisation, or a sculpture.

Performing [or Exhibiting] refers to performing [or exhibiting] an existing work, a process that calls upon the interpretive or re-creative skills of the students.

Responding refers to observing, describing, analyzing, and evaluating works of art. (p i)

Students need the opportunity to engage in the creative process to develop their own work in the visual arts, to exhibit their work as a finished product, and to respond to their own works of art and to the work of others. Engaging in this process is what makes learning in the arts a serious endeavor that allows to student the opportunity to articulate and reflect on the experience and to share their perceptions with others.

Authentic assessment strategies that include each of these three components help students to reflect on what they learned, the skills they developed, and how they feel about what happened through the experience. The artwork that the student creates can be used to assess their understanding of the art process or the criteria established in the assignment or how effective the piece is in communicating visually. Exhibiting the work requires working with the piece until it is finished, deciding when it is finished, mounting the work for display, creating a title for the piece, and indicating the materials used for creating the piece. Responding to the work allows students the opportunity to use the arts vocabulary to describe what they see, the techniques that were used, and the feelings the image evokes, or to make a connection to an experience in their own lives. Moving toward student self-assessment in these areas is the desired outcome. The sample unit included in this chapter contains student-created and teacher-created assessment tools designed for students to reflect upon and evaluate their own art process. In summary, the arts provide numerous opportunities for highly effective teaching and learning across the curriculum and engage students in authentic experiences that are meaningful and active. The unit that follows focuses on the essential question, "How is art a part of my life?" and provides a framework for exploring the ideas discussed in this chapter.

References

Arts Education Partnership. (2004). *The arts and education: New opportunities for research.* Washington, DC: Arts Education Partnership.

Catterall, J.S. (2002). The arts and the transfer of learning. In R. Deasy (Ed.) *Critical links: Learning in the arts and student academic and social development.* Washington, DC: Arts Education Partnership.

Cornett, C. E. (2004). *Creating meaning through literature and the art: An integration resource for classroom teachers.* New Jersey: Merrill Prentice Hall.

Deasy, R. (Ed). (2002). *Critical links: Learning in the arts and student academic and social development.* Washington, DC: Arts Education Partnership.

Eisner, E. (2002). *The arts and the creation of mind.* New Haven, CT: Yale University.

Fiske, E. (Ed.). (2000). *Champions of change: The impact of the arts on learning.* Washington, DC: Arts Education Partnership and the President's Committee on the Arts and the Humanities.

Gardner, H. (1989). *To open minds: Clues to the dilemma of contemporary education.* New York: Basic Books.

Goodlad, J. (1992). Toward a place in the curriculum for the arts. In B. Reimer & R. Smith (Eds.), *The arts, education, and aesthetic knowing.* NSSE Yearbook. Chicago: University of Chicago Press.

Greene, M. (1995). *Releasing the imagination: Essays on education, the arts, and social change.* San Francisco: Jossey-Bass.

Hawai'i Alliance for Arts Education (2001). *An essential arts toolkit for the K-5 classroom teacher: Hawai'i fine arts grade level guide.* Honolulu, HI: Hawai'i Alliance for Arts Education.

Landau, B. M. (1999). *Practicing judicious discipline: An educator's guide to a democratic classroom, 3ʳᵈ Edition*. San Francisco: Caddo Gap Press.

Pistone, N. (2002). *Envisioning arts assessment: A process guide for assessing arts education in school districts and states*. Washington, DC: Arts Education Partnership and the Council of Chief State School Officers. Retrieved March 27, 2006, from http://www.aeparts.org/PDF%20Files/EnvArtsAssess.pdf

Persky, H. R., Snadene, B. A., & Askew, J. M. (1998). The NAEP 1997 Arts Report Card, (NECS 1999-486) Washington, DC: National Center for Education Statistics. Retrieved March 27, 2006, from http://nces.ed.gov/nationsreportcard//pdf/main1997/1999486.pdf (p i-ii)

Stevenson, L. M., & Deasy, R. J. (2005). *Third space: When learning matters*. Washington, DC: Arts Education Partnership.

Tomlinson, C. A., & McTighe, J. (2006). *Integrating differentiated instruction and understanding by design: Connecting content and kids*. Alexandria, VA: Association for Supervision and Curriculum Development.

Wachowiak, F., & Clements, R. D. (2006). *Emphasis art: A qualitative art program for elementary and middle schools*, 8ᵗʰ edition. Boston: Pearson Education.

Judicious Classrooms at Holiday Times

Barbara Landau

How teachers address religion can help or hinder creating an atmosphere of respect and equity in the classroom. Students have the right to their free exercise of religious beliefs and the government, in this case public school teachers, must refrain from establishing religion or, to put another way, must keep from advancing one religious point of view. For example, a student who is silently praying before a meal or a test is exercising her First Amendment right to religious expression while a teacher who devotes class time to making Christmas decorations is violating First Amendment protections from the establishment of religion because the activity promotes one religious point of view.

While to some the act of maintaining this balance seems an impossibly difficult task, the Supreme Court has developed succinct language to guide educators in their practices. They advocate a standard of "wholesome neutrality," an almost lyrical phrase. This posture of neutrality is not one of disinterest or disaffection but rather a professional stance in which all perspectives are equally appreciated and no one perspective is presented as being more acceptable than another.

When planning activities related to religious holidays, three questions can help all teachers determine if what they are preparing to do meets the standard of being wholesomely neutrality. The three questions are commonly known as the "Lemon Test," a test developed as part of the findings in a Supreme Court case (*Lemon v. Kurtzman*) to determine what does and what does not constitute establishment of religion.

The first question is, does the activity being planned promote or prohibit religion? It should do neither of those things. Having students count up how many toys Santa has in his sleigh, has more to do with promoting one religious perspective than it does with teaching math computation skills. For those children who do not celebrate Christmas, the activity is forcing them to engage in a lesson that runs contrary to their family values.

On the other hand, if teachers ask children to draw a favorite activity during the month of December and some children draw a sledding scene, some draw a vacation scene, some draw a Nativity Scene and others draw a Menorah—all of that is ok. Religion has not been promoted or prohibited by asking students to engage in this art activity. In fact, teachers are doing exactly what the Constitution and the Supreme Court want us to do, that is to act in a wholesomely neutral manner. With the permission of the artists, all the student drawings can and should be displayed around the room.

Some teachers, who are trying not to violate the separation of church and state, inadvertently prohibit religion. For instance, some teachers reserve time for free reading during the day and encourage students to bring books from home or to select a book from the library. I have heard of situations that involve children bringing a Bible to read and being told they have to put it away and select another book. The reading time, however, is just like the art activity described above. The teacher has invited students to bring in a book with no other stated criteria. If students choose to read the Bible they are exercising their religious rights, but telling students they have to put that reading selection away has the effect of prohibiting that exercise.

Question number 2—does the activity have a legitimate secular purpose? When teaching language arts, art, history, health education, sex education, science, music, and social studies, it is inevitable that religion will be part of the conversation and it should be. Religion is intrinsic to our world cultures and we cannot provide our students with a clear picture of how societies are structured without discussing religion. We can certainly teach about religion but we need to take a neutral perspective and to make sure all religions are equally represented in classroom activities and discussions.

Accordingly, although "Christmas Around the World" would not be an appropriate Social Studies unit for the month of December, "Holidays Around the World" would be. It is important to give equal representation to all holidays. Ramadan, which can come anywhere from late fall to early spring depending on the lunar calendar, is too often ignored as a seasonal holiday but impacts Muslim students if they are fasting during the day. A unit on holidays around the world would help students understand why someone in their classroom or school needs to rest more often during that month and will probably not participate in snack time. Chanukah, a minor Jewish holiday, happens to fall around this time of year and still another holiday, Kwanza, an African-American holiday that teaches and celebrates core cultural values, comes at the end of December. None of these holidays have anything to do with Christmas, nor should they be compared to Christmas.

To ensure equity in a *Judicious Discipline* classroom, each holiday season should be approached with an educational, rather than celebratory, purpose. One way to practice equity would be to invite all parents who are interested to come in and share their special family customs that surround these various holidays. Too often, Jewish parents are invited in to explain their "different" holiday. A *Judicious Discipline* classroom would have all parents visiting to discuss their family's celebrations. Protestants, Catholics, Moslems, Buddhists, Jews, etc., should each be invited and provided an equal opportunity to talk about how their family celebrates a holiday.

The decorations that are on display should similarly serve the purpose of a wholesomely neutral education. If teachers want to teach a unit called "Holidays Around the World," then it would be entirely appropriate for the class bulletin boards to contain pictures and information related to each of the holidays included in the study. On the other hand, classrooms that feature Santa, reindeers, elves, and one menorah tucked away in the corner of the room are classrooms that fail to embrace the spirit of equity, fairness, and respect for all.

Religion is a natural part of the curriculum. It is interwoven throughout all cultures, it is a theme that runs through much of our literary and musical heritage, and it is a predominant topic in philosophy. Rather than fearing its presence in our curriculum, we should naturally reach out and embrace its potential influence. Some judicious schools understand that religion can play a part in establishing a tone for an in-school detention room. Such rooms can be decorated with sayings from Gandhi, Jesus, Helen Keller, Mohammed, Buddha, Rachel Carson, Martin Luther King, Moses, Nelson Mandela, and others who have contributed to the moral conversation of our world societies. The presence of so many diverse voices all speaking about the value of truth, honesty, respect, and responsibility creates a powerful montage and represents the essence of what it means to integrate religious messages into a bulletin board display that serves a legitimate secular purpose.

The third question is—does the activity represent a significant government entanglement in religion? For everyday school purposes, teachers should interpret "entanglement" to mean how much class time is invested in activities that promote one religious perspective. If the two or three weeks of December that precede the Winter Break are taken up with holiday assemblies devoted primarily to Christmas, rehearsals for Christmas music concerts, decorating halls and classrooms with Christmas-related themes, and making Christmas gifts for family members, it is easy to see that the level of entanglement is inappropriate for meeting the standard of equity and wholesome neutrality. With all the state and federal requirements for teaching required curricula and test preparation, spending so much of that precious class time on activities that do not protect the First Amendment rights of all students is hard to justify.

While classroom festivities may hold pleasant associations for the educators who plan them, what is often absent from their considerations is the sense of isolation experienced by children whose families do not celebrate the holiday being observed. These children are left to decide if they will participate in activities they do not personally value or remove themselves from the classroom and their peers, an act which only emphasizes their differences.

Classroom parties typically reduce religions to their most superficial aspects and marginalize the role religion can potentially play in the lives of students. Holidays become more a matter of getting gifts than significant opportunities to explore faith and culture. So what does all of this mean in practical terms? Here a few basic guidelines to be used along with the Lemon Test.

1. Use holiday-related activities to teach about all cultural groups during the course of the school year, not just in December. This does not mean making fortune cookies for Chinese New Year, but rather it means engaging in studies of Chinese cultures, or any other cultures. The studies should have depth and require students to engage in activities that broaden their understanding of world perspectives. A celebration of the Chinese New Year might well be part of a unit on China, and culminate with a festival that includes foods authentic to various Chinese cultures.

2. Honor all groups, especially those represented in your classroom. Do not treat some groups as "different" or their holidays as "exotic" while other holidays and groups are thought of as "normal."

3. Do not assume everyone from the same ethnic group celebrates holidays in the same way. A colleague of mine told me that he once taught in a high school that required Jewish students to show that their families had acquired tickets to attend High Holy Day services. If students could produce the tickets, they could be excused from school for the New Year and Day of Atonement observances. It is impossible to imagine that Christian chil-

43

dren would ever have to prove that they would attend church on Christmas in order to be excused from school. It is not the business of school officials to question how any family observes a religious holiday. Members of all cultural groups must be treated with equal respect and understanding.

4. Economic equity also becomes an issue related to holiday celebrations. Gift exchanges can be terribly difficult for the student whose caregivers do not have enough money to pay the heating or water bill. A student of mine once told me about a mother of one of her students who decided to not buy her full allotment of food stamps because she had to use some money to purchase a gift for her child's classroom gift exchange. Teachers need to carefully consider the tensions placed on families when trinkets that will be quickly discarded anyway are required for a class party.

Certainly the common values we all share as a society are reflected in the belief systems of the world's religions and a classroom built on wholesome neutrality would be an environment in which children can explore similarities as well as the differences all year long, ultimately finding value in both.

Making Schools Safe and Welcoming for LGBT Students

Bonnie Tinker

The first day of school! I still remember the excitement of returning to school in the fall. Everything was new: new shoes, a new notebook, and pencils that still had both a point and an eraser. There were best friends to share the excitement of getting ready for the new year, old classmates who lived further away who would now be with me everyday. The air was crisp and filled with new possibilities.

As a parent I shared my children's excitement about each new school year, and dutifully took their picture of the first day of every school year until they were so old that they ordered me to stop. But as a parent, the excitement—and relief that they would be back to a structured and productive existence—was always tempered with an underlying fear.

I am a lesbian parent, and I never could be sure of what disaster might befall our children when they went to school. The first child I sent off to school, my daughter, was adopted. But in those days, 1976, a legal adoption was not possible. I had no papers, no birth certificate, no medical records, and no way to get them. She had known me as her mother all of her life, but the law did not recognize me as her legal parent. We carefully interviewed schools until we found one that seemed safe. Ironically, it was a Catholic school that was most prepared to accept a child

45

with two mothers. Of course the Sister who was the principal, a good woman, asked us not to let the other parents know we were lesbians as that might have "caused trouble."

Soon I had a second child to be concerned about. My partner Sara's son was already ten when we got together. I didn't really have any responsibility for his schooling because in 1977 there was really no way to describe who I was in his life, so I stayed out of it. It was our own self-imposed version of a "don't ask don't tell" policy. The school didn't ask and we didn't tell. We thought we were protecting him, but when he grew up he told us that our silence didn't stop the teasing. It just added to the shame.

Our baby was another story. He was younger, born in 1983 and I was braver. I was out to the school staff. I asked him if he was afraid to let his friends know that his mom was a lesbian. He said, "I'm not worried about my friends. I know them. It's their parents I'm worried about." He had good reason to be worried about other parents. When he was five he lost his very best friend; she was no longer allowed to play with him because we were lesbians. He said to me, "I know how to solve this problem. If my life were in a garbage can there wouldn't be a problem."

Many years later, when he was a junior in high school, he told this story to Barbara Walters on a 20/20 program about kids with gay parents. She asked him how he felt about it and he said, "Little kids aren't supposed to be that sad."

He's right, little kids aren't supposed to feel that sad. They aren't supposed to think that their lives belong in the garbage can. But little kids all over the world know those feelings if their parents are lesbian, gay, bi or trans (LGBT), or if they themselves are LGBT. They are not excited about going to school. They are terrified.

It doesn't have to be that way. There are a few school districts, like ours in Portland, Oregon, that have made great strides toward making schools safe for all students, and providing a supportive learning environment for kids from all kinds of families, including LGBT kids and families. These schools did not change by accident or luck. Parents and educators identified the ways that bias based on sexual orientation and gender identity is institutionally taught and perpetuated. They worked for change on both a personal and an institutional level, and more remains to be done.

Portland was not the first school district to begin making changes, but it is the one I know best so I will use it to illustrate some of the problems and approaches to solving these problems. The initial problem we faced was visibility. Students, parents, and teachers were all afraid to be out to each other and to anyone else. Teachers were afraid they would be fired if they came out, or even if it was alleged that they were gay. They were right to assume this; that is what had always happened to LGBT teachers in the past. They had no contract protection. [Ed. note: Even a tenured teacher can be fired for what is deemed to be immoral behavior.] It is difficult for teachers to be very visible, much less vocal, if they don't have contract protection. In Portland the teacher's union finally gained protection from discrimination based on sexual orientation. The Cascade union of Educators was formed in 1986. They met in private homes and were mostly closeted on the job. By some good fortune I was invited to a meeting of this group the summer before my daughter entered high school because of work I was doing to create an LGBT program for the American Friends Service Committee. At that meeting I met the teacher who would become my daughter's home room teacher.

That one meeting probably did more to help my daughter stay in school and graduate than anything else I could have done. This teacher was aware of an effort to deny certain special needs services to our daughter because one of the other teachers said, "her only problem is that she has a lesbian mother." I had to petition the State superintendent of schools to get the services she needed, but without inside information about the bias it would have been much more difficult. I cannot say enough in praise of LGBT teachers, and teachers who are LGBT supportive, who come out at school. School is always a safer place when students know there are teachers who understand and value them.

The teachers also did something that was immeasurably valuable to all of the LGBT kids in Portland schools. In 1990 with the support of the superintendent, they formed an internal Diversity Task Force to look at ways the district could become more supportive of LGBT kids. Two members of this group were lesbian parents. Through this group they created a training program for staff, and the district offered this training to all levels of staff for a number of years until the funding dried up.

Parents, those who were LGBT, were wary of coming out because they were afraid they could lose custody of their children, and they were afraid their children would be tormented by their peers and treated unfairly by teachers. These were reasonable fears. Parents who come out are still losing custody of their children in many, if not most, jurisdictions in the United States. Most large urban areas are now islands of safety, but even they cannot protect children from teasing. I don't have any statistical studies, but I would bet that the vast majority of kids with LGBT parents can tell of at least one incident where they were teased because of their parents.

Parents of LGBT kids often are reluctant for their kids to come out. Although teens in some supportive urban areas may tell their parents when they realize they are not straight, this is still an act of tremendous courage. Most of these kids are in high school; they are not likely to want their parents to get involved with the school even if they are supportive. The key to bringing together parents is to bring together LGBT parents and parents of LGBT kids. The former know who they are when their kids are in kindergarten, so they can work for systemic change from the very beginning. Parents of LGBT kids are likely to be older and already know the ropes of working with a school system.

I started organizing other parents when our youngest son was in fourth grade. That just happened to be 1992, the year Oregon faced Ballot Measure 9, one of the first virulent, all purpose anti-gay measures to hit the state.

I began simply by putting an announcement in the PTA (Parent Teachers' Association) newsletter that was sent to all parents. The announcement said: "Lesbian and gay parents, and those who support our children, are invited to a meeting. Contact Bonnie." And I put my phone number in. I did not put my last name in, at our son's request. I learned from the school counselor that the principal considered not running the announcement. It's one time my family name came in handy. My siblings were the plaintiffs in *Tinker vs. the Des Moines Public School* board. The counselor told the principal, "I think you'd better run it or Bonnie will sue you." She ran it, and later became very supportive.

From this announcement I did find a few other lesbian parents in the school as well as several straight parents willing to join. The school counselor told me that my son's teacher was a closeted gay man, and that the school social worker had a gay son. With this little support group we accomplished several things:

· With their encouragement I spoke to the PTA and they took a position opposing the anti-gay legislation (Measure 9).

· The new Superintendent of Portland Public Schools, John Bierwirth, also had a child in this school. He saw that other parents in his child's school supported LGBT people and families and he let us know that he supported us.

· We put together a network of supportive parents so that when the closeted teacher "came out" there was already parent support for him. This undercut opposition from other parents.

· We created an educational panel presentation to talk to the staff at our school and others in the district.

· We sponsored and gained approval of a state-wide PTA resolution that opposed discrimination based on sexual orientation, and opposed all legislative attempts to suppress discussion of family diversity. This gave the PTA the platform to oppose all subsequent anti-gay ballot measures.

Eventually one of the panel members, Joseph Tam, ran for the school board and won. He pushed for a school board resolution baring military recruiters from all Portland Public Schools because they discriminated based on sexual orientation. He also invited us to form a "parent involvement group" similar to the groups for Latino/a parents, Tag parents, etc. In response to this invitation we created the Sexual Minority Parents Advisory Group (SMPAG). This gave us a direct *institutional* connection to the top level of administrators, including the superintendent, which continued as different people came in to fill various administrative positions. It also gave us an organizational connection to a staff group, the Diversity Task Force that had been quietly working internally to district staff with basic information about the challenges facing LGBT students.

Several years into this process our youngest son, Alex, again provided motivation to push for a significant institutional change. When one of his sixth grade classmates teased him about having a lesbian mom (the kid was mad because Alex's race car had just beat his race car), Alex got into a physical fight. Both boys were suspended, but neither of them said anything about the cause of the fight. I picked Alex up and was talking to him about the evils of fighting when he finally told me the cause of the fight. Over the years I have learned that it is common for kids with LGBT parents to withhold information about how they are affected by the teasing at school, and this was one of the incidents that taught me this lesson.

I was furious that this factor had not been considered, or passed on to me. It's possible that none of the teachers knew what was going on, but it's also possible they didn't recognize the impact on Alex. In any case, I called the school and spoke with the vice principal when the principal wasn't available. In telling her I wanted a meeting with the principal, I said "Alex was fighting and he should have been suspended. And a hate crime happened in your school and I want to know if the principal has been suspended."

Fortunately I had calmed down by the time I went, with an advocate from our panel, to talk to the principal, Peter Hamilton. He had really not thought much about the problem of homophobia in his school, but was concerned. In the course of our discussion I pointed out that one of the problems in ending homophobic attacks was that there was no school-wide policy against discrimination based on sexual orientation. He responded with immediate support by writing a letter that went out to all parents saying the school would not tolerate homophobic remarks. He also later became Chair of the middle school principals' group, and used this position to encourage other principals to consider the needs of LGBT students and kids with LGBT parents.

I also talked to Steve Fulmer, a gay man who worked in the district office, about the policy problem. He was already working on this issue and had compiled a table showing that district policies against discrimination were inconsistent. Some covered discrimination based on race in certain situations, and others covered sexual discrimination, for example. Working in an advisory capacity to the School Board, he presented a table showing the complex inconsistencies. The School board passed a new blanket anti-discrimination policy that included sexual orientation and gender identity.

Peter Hamilton also helped us by showing the *Love Makes a Family* phototext exhibit (produced by Family Diversity Projects). At this time, it was still very controversial to share photos and stories about LGBT families in the classroom or even in more public spaces in schools (libraries, the hallway). I realized that one of the most damaging things happening to our students was never hearing any mention of families like theirs at school. For kids with LGBT parents, this meant that they were invisible and, de facto, devalued. For LGBT students this meant that they never saw images of people like themselves as parents. They did not have a vision of how they could become adults with families of their own. I was determined that Alex—the only one of our children remaining in public school—would see images of LGBT families in his school before he graduated. It had occurred to me that the absence of any reflection of their families in school creates an unequal learning environment. I had talked to several lawyers about the similarities to the *Brown v. Board of Education* (1954) decision. Studies building that case showed, among other things, the damage to Black children when they did not see themselves reflected in educational materials. Black children who are fed an educational diet of White Dick, Jane, and Sally with their mother in an apron and their father in a business suit internalize a message of second-class citizenship. So do students who have a mother and a mother or a father and a father.

The images and stories in schools affect the success of students. During the 1992 Ballot Measure 9 campaign in Oregon the Oregon Citizen's Alliance (OCA) claimed that we would want lesbian and gay books in school libraries. People running our campaign opposing the ballot measure—I don't believe any of them were LGBT parents—said that wasn't true, that the only way books got into the school library was through an approved list and we weren't pushing for inclusion of LGBT books.

I took a different approach. I thought we should tell the truth and responded by saying, "Yes, we do want books that show our families. Our children are already in school and they have the same right as other children to see their families reflected in the books they read in school." I don't accept bogie man status because someone wants to give it to me in a political campaign. I am not some creepy "homosexual" of perverse political fantasies. I am just another parent trying to do what is best for my family. I have always found that straight parents respond to this concern. Once they understand that children are being hurt, they change.

We did manage some changes before Alex graduated. The photo text exhibit was shown in his school and others. The Portland Public School District sent a letter out to all parents from SMPAG letting them know that we existed and including a list of resources useful to all parents. They sent a letter to all faculty encouraging them to remember that not all children have one mother—or any mother—on Mother's Day, and reminding them to think of lesbian and gay students when Valentine's Day festivities took over the schools each year.

The groups we created to effect these changes did not continue. Both the staff group and the parent group are gone due in part to budget cuts, but also due to success. The culture of Portland Public Schools changed. Most high schools and many middle schools now have "Gay Straight Alliances (GSAs)." Staff are aware of teasing based on sexual orientation and most can be relied upon to interrupt it. Several years ago I heard of a middle school aid who told two girls that they shouldn't hold hands because it was wrong. The principal announced at an all-school meeting that such bias would not be tolerated.

We have reached a point of tolerance, but there is more to be done for our students to feel fully included. It's not just up to the schools to end discrimination. As long as same-sex couples are not allowed legal recognition of their marriages, our children will get the message that we—and they—are second class citizens. Schools can't change this, but they can treat LGBT parents with the same respect given to opposite sex parents. Laws often follow the wisdom of the people. Schools can recognize the fact that we are families, and can incorporate this recognition into all aspects of school policy and curriculum.There is a new generation of children with lesbian, gay, bisexual and trans parents. Population studies are woefully lacking, but I would guess there is at least one child in almost every public school in the country who lives with two mothers or two fathers. As these parents are encouraged to be out in school, they will provide guidance for the next level of policy and curriculum changes that move us from tolerance to inclusion.

And the need for tolerance in schools is more than just a good idea. A disproportionate percentage of homeless teens are sexual minorities unable to live with their families of origin. In most countries in the world, same-sex couples are denied the right to form a family. As of March, 2006, only one state, Massachusetts, provides legal recognition of same sex marriage. Until very recently any parent who came out could expect to lose custody, and possibly visitation, of their children. Numerous states expressly forbid adoption of children by same sex couples (or even individuals who are not self avowed heterosexuals). There have been legislative attempts to deny lesbian women the right to conceive through insemination.

When we really start looking at schools, we see many ways in which schools teach heterosexuality, or set a standard that heterosexuality is preferable. Kindergarteners will spontaneously play dress up as brides and grooms; children are ridiculed if they don't take the "appropriate" role when playing house.

Prom Queens are paired with Prom Kings; the left-over home-coming princesses are given male escorts. Most novels read in literature classes are built around male/female romances. I have met with school administrators and been told that the reason a child with lesbian parents was teased was because he told his classmates his mother was a lesbian. It was his own fault that he did not remain invisible.

Social change is a cumbersome process. People who understand the need for change also understand the enormity of the problem. The first step toward change is to believe that one person can make a difference. The second is to listen for the voices of support and gather them together. Social change is not done *for* someone else; it empowers the disenfranchised, moving the marginalized into a position to lead. There are three critical elements to creating social change: constituency support, institutional change, and public education. If the affected constituency does not have support, they are not in a position to inform and lead the change. If change does not happen on an institutional level, it will not endure. If the general public does not support the change, they will effectively undermine it.

The first step in supporting sexual minority people is to encourage visibility and recognition of our families. Sexual minority people have been particularly oppressed by exclusion from the institutions of *the family*. Although there is evidence that some Western societies made room for families headed by same-sex couples, there has been active social and legal rejection of homosexuality for generations. Historically individuals who came out have been subject to prison and even death. They were almost guaranteed ostracism from their family of origin. This still happens, even in the United States. A disproportionate percentage of homeless teens are sexual minorities unable to live with their families of origin. In most countries in the world, same-sex couples are denied the right to form a family. Until very recently any parent who came out could expect to lose custody, and possibly visitation, of their children.

Students who are LGBT or who come from sexual minority families are supported and provided an equal educational environment when schools support them. Enlightened attitudes can reveal themselves through:

· Staff benefits that are extended to opposite sex partners should be extended to same sex partners.

· Ensuring that heterosexual staff are allowed to keep pictures of their partners on their desks, the same is true for people with same sex partners.

· Elementary schoolteachers recognizing different family structures by referring to "parents" or "responsible adults" instead of to "your mother and father."

· Children being asked to talk about their families through the use of open ended questions such as "Who do you live with?" instead of "Who are your mother and father?"

· School forms replacing "parent" with "responsible adult."

· Text books and books in school libraries that reflect the diversity of family structures that actually exist in our society—nuclear families with only one mother and one father, single parent families, grandparents raising children, foster families, blended post divorce families, and families with two mothers or two fathers.

· When making cards or presents for parents or guardians during holidays that recognize family configurations are different. Students may need to make two, or even three; Mother's Day cards for example.

· Sex education classes that include information about same-sex relationships.

· Student romances, the precursor to young people thinking about and planning future families, are equally supported without regard to the sex or gender of the partners. Rules of conduct for couples should apply equally without regard for the sex or gender of the parties. Dances and proms should be open to all couples without regard to sex, gender or race.

· Letting students know they are in safe space by posting signs, pink triangle, or rainbows in classrooms.

· Discussing anti-gay ballot measures in civics classes. Teachers need to set expectations for the tone of the discussion. Respect and tolerance must be the basic expectations. Otherwise real emotional damage can be done to some students. For example, if an anti-gay group proposes that lesbians and gays not be allowed to adopt children this will affect all lesbian and gay students, all children with lesbian or gay parents, and especially all children adopted by lesbian or gay parents.

· Discussion of legal recognition of same sex marriages as not just a political controversy. It affects all children living with lesbian or gay parents, and it also directly affects lesbian and gay students who want to marry, and students with lesbian or gay relatives. The very personal nature of this topic can be acknowledged and support provided through selection of outside speakers, and again, ground rules for respectful discussions.

Institutional structures, intentionally or not, can perpetuate discrimination. Beyond providing direct support to students, we can look for ways to remove the structural supports for discrimination:

· All school non-discrimination policies should include sexual orientation and gender identity. Organizations which violate this policy have no place in schools. Unfortunately, the military and the Boy Scouts have been given special rights (through the "No Child Left Behind" legislation) to be in schools in defiance of non-discrimination policies. There are ways schools can limit the impact of this discrimination through building use and distribution of literature policies.

· Dress codes should not be sex specific.

· Employee contracts should protect employees from discrimination based on sexual orientation or gender identity.

· Administrators should abide by and enforce laws giving students freedom of speech and the right to assemble. Students and teachers have a right to discuss sexual orientation. If this right is violated, supportive community members should intervene.

· If there are school clubs, sexual minority students have a right to form a club such as a Gay Straight Alliance.

· Unfortunately, churches have been the primary organizational vehicle for propagating discrimination based on sexual orientation. Students have a right to be free from religious discrimination in school. Churches, especially those that preach or practice discrimination based on race, sex, or sexual orientation, have no business having any official presence in public schools.

· Studies show that students whose parents are involved in schools have a better chance at success. Sexual minority parents can be encouraged to form parent involvement groups with direct access to administrators to identify any problems with discrimination.

· In-service education for administrators and all staff with direct student contact can help staff recognize and respond appropriately to incidents of discrimination they observe.

· Approved book and video lists should consider diversity of sexual orientation along with other educational concerns.

Many school districts that have adopted the kinds of changes suggested above have gone through a period of fear or actual public controversy ranging from contentious school board meetings to picketers with ghastly messages of Hell illustrated by leaping flames. Lasting change requires an ongoing plan for public education.

The simplest form of education is personal story presentations that I've come to call "gay on display." This was the one of the first formats for public education, and continues to be useful today. In most large urban area there are LGBT organizations that will provide speakers to talk to classes, civic groups, or churches about the experience of being gay. Speakers share their own stories and cover basic information such as "it's not contagious," "we're born this way," "teasing hurts," and "job discrimination is wrong." Speakers will also give basic information about terms used to talk about sexual orientation and gender identity and ideas about how people can let LGBT people know they are in a safe environment. These panels were pioneered by PFLAG (Parents Family and Friends of Lesbians and Gays). Today presentations often include a sexual minority parent, a young adult raised by sexual minority parents, and a parent of a sexual minority youth.

Ironically, anti-gay ballot measures have provided one of the best opportunities for public education. Before such measures in 1992 in Oregon and Colorado triggered a continuing wave, it was very difficult to initiate any public discussion of sexual minority concerns, and almost impossible to talk to students. With the ballot measures, however, it has became a matter of public policy and schools were anxious to have speakers "on both sides" of the issue. As a result of these discussions, and increasing visibility in the media, polls show that younger generations are much more accepting of differences in sexual orientation and gender identity.

My own experience with our children and their friends when very young suggests that children are naturally open to these differences and only become judgmental as they learn social sex role expectations. One difficulty in using the forum presented by ballot measures is that the political arena is naturally adversarial. Many people caught up in these campaigns are really interested in discussing the issues in depth, but campaigns from both sides try to limit the information to carefully chosen sound bites.

Engaging in genuine dialog about very controversial topics is difficult, but it can be done if we switch from an "attack and defend mentality" to a "getting to know you" approach. My own work is now focused on helping people learn how to engage in constructive dialogs with family, friends, neighbors, church groups, and fellow students.

I just read in *Newsweek* (February 6, 2006) that through evangelical college debate training, "Policy debate on the college level has become a rapid-fire verbal assault." Jerry Falwell says, "We are training debaters who can perform assault ministry." I'm not surprised. I've been on the receiving end of this "assault ministry" for the past 14 years. Cultural war has been declared upon lesbian, gay, bi and trans people. Make no mistake, this same war has been declared upon anyone who does not adhere to the strict religious tenets of the cultural warriors. Anyone who has ever considered sexual infidelity or divorce should take note. The real question for schools is not what students will be taught to believe, but are schools safe for students who do not conform to the moral mandates of fundamentalist religions (curiously, different brand of religious fundamentalism tend to share the same basic prejudices)?

War, cultural or physical, does not make school safe for anyone. Lesbian, gay, bi and trans students, and children with LGBT parents, are in a war zone in most schools in the United States. It is the role of educators and parents to take the war out of our schools, to make schools "hate free zones" where ideas and natural differences can be expressed with mutual respect. We can do this by protecting students who are the targets of verbal, physical, and social assaults with direct action and institutional changes. We can assure that peace, another word for safety, prevails by sharing our stories and engaging in earnest dialog about our differences.

Resource List

GLSEN
Love Makes A Family

Massachusetts Department of Education
OSSCC
Safe Schools Coalition
Vancouver, British Columbia, Group
Women's Educational Media

Inclusive Environment:
Educating All Students in General Education Classrooms

Younghee Kim

The real voyage of discovery consists not in seeking new land-
scapes but in having *new eyes.*

—Marcel Proust

What It Means To Be Inclusive

In a warm and caring classroom, the teacher tries hard to
know the students and understand their special needs and unique
strengths. With keen observations, daily interactions, and genuine dialogue, the teacher comes to "know" students by heart.
With warm-hearted attention from the teacher, students feel
connected, empowered, accepted, and valued, therefore more
likely to try out challenging tasks and to do well.

Teachers who are attuned to caring for students with various
backgrounds truly try to understand and get to know the students
early on. These teachers talk to the students' previous teachers,
communicate frequently with the parents, and try to find out what
is needed, what is most interesting, and what works best for their
students. Teachers intentionally include various community-
building activities for students from the beginning of the school
year. They know that a comfortable, open, and warm classroom
environment is the foundation for learning (See Figure 1).

The teacher's role expands further to find the genuine

Figure 1.
Characteristics of an Inclusive, Authentic, and Judicious Classroom.

	Authentic Curriculum— Providing Exciting, Fun, Engaging Learning	Judicious Actions—Building Positive, Encouraging Environment
Teacher has or provides	Creative, inviting instruction *Judicious Discipline* Highly engaging curriculum Flexible but firm deadlines Differentiated, individualized instruction Democratic management Explorative hands-on activities Problem-solving tactics Higher-level thinking activities Nature observation, outdoor science Students-centered and -focused Fair expectations for all students Intellectually challenging and socially-engaging lesson planning Student interest reflected curriculum Simulation of real life issues Connection to the real world Performanced-based assessments Strong literacy-based learning Alternative learning stations	Well organized with high expectations Patient and encoraging manner Good listening skills, sense of humor Warm and caring demeanor Individual connections with students Sensitive and supportive Responsive and proactive Flexible thinking and planning Fair evaluation, open communication Respectuful of student opinions Modeling of ethical moral actions Reflectve decision-making Social-critical thinking Assessment of student's prior knowledge and background experiences Positive and cheerful demeanor Tuned for student needs and talents Welcomes diversity Promotes multicultural perspectives Smiles and laughs often
Students are or have	Basic needs met (fun, power, freedom, love and belonging, and survival) Creative and curious for learning High self-esteem and self-efficacy Freedom of choices, exploration Creative and critical thinking Higher level of thinking skills Cooperative learning skills Communication skills Social critical thinking Service learning, contributing Judicious and democratic mind Constitutional understanding	Hard working, serious for learning Highly motivated and engaged Ownership of their learning and work Healthy friendship with peers Supportive and respectful of each other Helping out one another Teamwork and group collaboration Positive attitudes towards each other Shared leadership, good listening Actively participating Though-through decision making Volunteer for classroom chores Reflective journals
Social, Physical Environment	Student work and arts well displayed Regular classroom meetings Respect student-made classroom rules Real life examples and learning (field trips, explorations, arts, music, guest presenters, dramas, creative movements) Chaotic and yet orderly Organized, well-planned for access Home work supports Community-based, service learning Motivation for life-long learning	Intentionally inviting classroom Trust and respect Strong relationships with everyone Good sense of humor Cheerful, noisy, joyful atmosphere Encouraging, positive relationships Forgiving, graceful attitudes Shared responsibilities and roles Close communication with parents Responsibile decisions and actions Smiles and laughter Celebration of learning

interests of students and supports them not only academically but also socially and emotionally. The strong relationships between the teacher and the students can extend to be a model for forming close peer relationships. The whole classroom develops an accepting and encouraging environment. It is an affective curriculum that the teacher implicitly creates to make feel valued and trusted in the learning environment. With closer understanding of students personally and culturally, the teacher can intuitively guide the students toward the desire for life-long learning (Wink, 2000). In a judiciously inclusive classroom, everyone becomes genuine learning partners for one another.

Both regular and special education teachers have been encountering increasing challenges in serving students with diverse needs who are included in general classrooms. The term "diverse" in this text spans the spectrum of skills, prior experiences, cultures, languages, ethnic and racial backgrounds, identified disabilities, socio economic status, social emotional aspects and any identified or unidentified needs or risks accounting for any delay in learning.

Teachers need to provide a continuum of services for all the diversity present in all classroom activities as much as possible. Inclusion, therefore, must be a systematic approach incorporating "individually appropriate" "socio-culturally compatible" and "linguistically meaningful" instruction. (Coutinho & Repp, 1999, p. 78). This may seem to be a daunting challenge. But it can also be an exciting opportunity for the teachers, including both regular and special education, to collaborate in creating meaningful instruction for individual students at their developmentally appropriate levels.

Why Inclusion Is a Good Fit with *Judicious Discipline*

Inclusion shares many important assumptions with *Judicious Discipline* in that they both support equal and fair access to education for all children. In academically diverse and inclusive classrooms, teachers should differentiate instruction to provide responsive, engaging learning experiences for students who differ in "readiness, interest, and learning profile" (Tomlinson,

1999; Tomlinson et al., 2004). In a *Judicious Discipline* classroom, it is important for students to learn to be citizens of democracy by living in classrooms that are organized democratically, meaning that they have the equal right to participate in learning activities, choose materials and books of their interests, and take on roles and responsibilities as equal members of the classroom. Table 1 shows how the two concepts, Inclusion and *Judicious Discipline*, share similar philosophy and practices.

In order to build a classroom that is both inclusive and judicious, the teacher will need to encourage students to participate in creating the environment together.

As mentioned above, there are several important aspects in designing inclusive, judicious classrooms that include building strong relationship with students, adapting curriculum and arranging the environment to meet the needs of all students, planning and facilitating authentic learning experiences, and collaborating closely with special education teachers and parents. Figure 2 describes a well-balanced judicious, inclusive, and authentic classroom encompassing all these aspects.

Curriculum Adaptations and Environmental Arrangements

Traditionally, teachers have been used to focusing on the

Table 1.
Similarities of Inclusive and Judicious Classrooms

Inclusive Classroom	Judicious Classroom
Everyone is included/meaningful participation	Everyone is equally and fairly treated.
Different abilities or disabilities are welcomed.	Everyone has the right to agree or disagree.
Everyone has the right for free, appropriate, public education—Due process for hearing	Everyone has the right for equal education—Due process for appeal, freedom of expression
Appropriate roles w/ strengths & special needs	Everyone has the rights and responsibilities.
Least restrictive environment	Most democratic environment/shared leadership
Students w/ Individual Educational Plan (IEP)	Practical, individualized, ownership for learning
Fair rules for all with/without disabilities.	Rules based on the Compelling State Interests

Figure 2.
A Well-Balanced Inclusive Classroom Environment

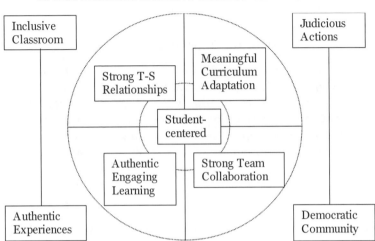

problems of the students first: "What is wrong with Kate?" "What's the problem with Johnny, he just cannot sit still?" "Sammy always looks for a trouble." "Timmy doesn't finish his work in time." "Lee never brings homework on time." "Betty must stay in recess to finish the worksheet, otherwise she'll never do it."

However, in proactive and responsive classrooms, teachers look for possibilities and potentials in each student first. "Kate didn't look happy this morning. Something must have happened before school." "Johnny likes to stand during circle time, so let him stand as long as he doesn't distract other kids' listening." "Sammy seems bored during reading. Something can be adapted to interest him." "Timmy gets distracted during desk work, maybe he can work in a trio group." "Lee seems having difficulty bringing his homework to school. I will need to talk to the parents for some ideas." "Betty needs much more time to finish tasks than other kids. I wonder what might help her focus better." By intentionally looking for strengths, potentials, motivators, talents, or interests within each student, teachers can find and emphasize what students can do rather than what they cannot do. From these questions and reflections, teachers can develop about how to adapt instructional approaches.

Asking the Important Questions

In the spirit of equitably addressing all learning needs, teachers must begin with the assessment of all the students' prior knowledge and skills. The information will help to ensure students will get what they need in order to successfully master information without having to repeat information they already have. Once teachers have done pre-assessments, they can use the information to systematically differentiate instruction to meet each individual learning styles and needs. But this is only the first step.

To create inclusive, judicious, and meaningful learning opportunities, teachers also need to ask themselves some critical questions: What is the enduring understanding? Why is it important to teach? How can it best be learned? How should I plan my teaching? How do I need to change to meet the needs of students with disabilities? How can I break down the steps for everyone to succeed? How can I arrange the environment for better access? What am I looking for in terms of outcomes from this unit? In what ways can the learning be most meaningful for each student?

Finally, after teaching the lesson, teachers may ask themselves the following questions: How did it go? What happened? How do I know that everyone understood the concept? How did I do it, and why? How should I do it differently next time to best reach this or that student? What worked and why? What did I learn from teaching this lesson? What did I learn about my students? Why did I do the way I did?

What Does the Classroom Look Like?

The physical classroom environment also plays a role in an inclusive, judicious classroom. Rooms should be visually interesting with plenty of displays including the student work, after they have given permission, and hands-on materials to tap on the student interests. Available materials should provide students with opportunities to explore their own interests, create art projects or performances, and see their work valued by the teacher.

Arranging the environment in an organized manner, both physically and socially, becomes critical in promoting the ways that work best for all students with different learning styles. This can be done by facilitating adequate time and access to supportive learning materials, diverse groupings, experiential learning centers, and varied seating arrangements. Such proactive planning supports judiciously well-organized environments and allows for students to have fair access and equal opportunity for learning.

Authentic Learning Experiences

Authentic learning means real-life based learning. Authentic activity based learning, because it is naturally motivating and engaging, is effective teaching practice and aligns with best practices for individual children with varying cognitive and affective styles and interests (Zimelman, Daniels, & Hyde, 2005). These activities emphasize higher-order thinking, and learning key concepts and principles in realistic applied settings. They also can model the principles of democracy in school as students gather in class meetings or small learning groups to discuss, brainstorm, debate, negotiate, evaluate, or synthesize with their peers in carrying out cooperative group projects in the interdependent learning community.

Teachers can vary the nature of the groupings according to skills, abilities, disabilities, characteristics, gender, talents, or developmental levels. During the process of learning, teachers need to observe the dynamics and group process to monitor and supervise the student progress and accomplishments. Teachers will record anecdotal, qualitative observations and descriptive evaluation of student growth, which will be included in formative, on-going assessments of students with timely feedback and eventually used for authentic, portfolio assessment for individual children when appropriate. These authentic experiences "foster deep and lasting learning for students with disabilities and gifts and talents" (Quindlen, 2006).

State standards or district learning benchmarks can be easily integrated in this type of holistic teaching and learning. Quindlen (2006) suggests "[k]eep it real!" when bringing classroom experiences to life for the students: "When students can see, touch or hear as they build knowledge, the lessons are lasting and meaningful" (p. 1). Some examples of authentic learning activities inside the classroom may include simulations, jeopardy games, mock history enactments, mock debate, process drama, story telling, autobiography writing, book club, workshops to learn new skills, performances for real audiences of parents, students at the same grade or different grade levels, or young children in the community, science fairs, school newspaper writing, planning for a book swap at the local library, and many more.

Authentic learning experiences can also occur outside the classroom. Teachers might want to initially take students into the community to explore interests, look for changes, identify things they think can be improved, or investigate services. If students want to enact some change, start with something manageable and affordable.

Teachers need to do extended planning ahead of time and assess student interests. This advance preparation will ensure students can research the necessary information, set their goals to work for, and identify resources from outside the classroom. [Ed. note: Betty Powers' Community Activity Plan would fit well with these ideas.]

Student interests in which projects to take on and how to manage them can be discussed in class meetings. This offers students genuine input into the process of determining their project and in goal setting to accomplish the project. This sort of community project is well aligned with the spirit of *Judicious Discipline* in terms of students becoming caring and contributing members of their society.

Team Collaboration:
Regular and Special Education Teacher, and the Parents

The inclusion movement has changed the role of the regular

classroom teacher as well as that of the special education teacher (Meyen, Vergason, & Whelan, 1996). As the effects of "pull-out" traditional services, taking out the student with disabilities from the regular classroom, are being reexamined (McWilliam, 1996), both regular and special pre-service teachers are increasingly being prepared to work in inclusive classrooms. Teachers are more prepared for professional collaboration because they need to seek support from each other. This trend leads the regular classroom teachers to work with the special education teachers so that students can be physically included with peers. In this "in-class" collaboration, the team teachers know the students with special needs, how to provide students with meaningful learning environments and how to better understand each other's instructional adaptations. Such cohesive collaboration can only support the student's success without being excluded or removed from home classroom.

Parents are also a vital part in this collaborative relationship. In truly meaningful partnerships with the parents, the teachers listen to the parents to understand their needs and desires for their child, remain open to alternative options, and are creative in meeting each individual child's unique needs. Parents are more likely able to stand for themselves when they see the professionals are genuinely interested in their child's well being. In such cases, there will be much less criticism, oppositional attitudes, restricted view points, or limited decision making, but more trustful, open, heartfelt, genuine, supportive, and respectful relationship centered around the student. This team approach aligns with *Judicious Discipline* in working together to advocate and protect the student's benefit for equal educational opportunity. Such collaboration becomes more powerful and productive as well as providing a relaxed and comfortable work place for everyone involved.

Summary

Several perspectives were discussed in this chapter in relation to including all students, with and without disabilities, in general authentic learning environments. Figure 1 lists some characteristics of an inclusive classroom that is authentic and promotes judicious learning for all the learners. Inclusion aligns with *Judicious Discipline* so every student, with or without disabilities, has the equal educational opportunities, and rights and responsibilities for learning in the most effective, authentic, and appropriate inclusive classroom. In such environments, "the real voyage of discovery" belongs to teachers as they develop new eyes and hearts for every child. By making a commitment to growth and improvement, a self-reflective teacher transforms the classroom into a judicious environment that includes everyone in life-long learning.

References

CEC Today. (March, 2006). Online CEC quarterly magazine. www.cecsped.org.

Coutinho, M. J., & Repp. A. C. (1999). *Inclusion: The integration of students with disabilities*. Belmont, CA: Wadsworth.

Lewis, R. B., & Doorlag, D. H. (2006). *Teaching special students in general education classrooms* (7th Ed.). Upper Saddle River, NJ: Prentice-Hall.

Landau, B. (2007). Practicing judicious discipline: An educator's guide to a democratic classroom (4th Ed.). San Francisco: Caddo Gap Press.

McWilliam, R. A. A. (1996). *Rethinking pull-out services in early intervention: A professional resource*. Baltimore, MD: Paul. H. Brookes.

Meyen, E. L., Vergason, G. A., & Whenlan, R. J. (Eds.) (1996). *Strategies for teaching exceptional children in inclusive settings*. Denver, CO: Love.

Quindlen, T. H. (2006). Authentic experiences foster deep and lasting learning for students with disabilities and gifts and talents. *CEC Today* (March, 2006).

Tate, M. (2003). *Worksheets don't grow dendrites: 20 instructional strategies that engage the brain*. Thousand Oaks, CA: Corwin Press.

Tomlinson, C. (1999). *The differentiated classroom: Responding to the needs of all learners*. Alexandria, VA: Association for Supervision and Curriculum Development.

Tomlinson, C. Brighton, C., Hertberg, H. Callahan, C., Moon, T., Brimijoin, K., Conover, L., & Reynolds, T. (2004). Differentiating instruction in response to student readiness, interest, and learning profile in academically diverse classrooms: A review of literature. *Journal for the Education of the Gifted, 27*, 119-145.

Wink, J. (2000). *Critical pedagogy: Notes from the real world* (2nd Ed.). New York: Longman.

Zemelman, S., Daniels, H. & Hyde, A. (1998, 2005). *Best practice: New standards for teaching and learning in America's schools* (2nd Ed.). Portsmouth, NH: Heineman.

Deliberately Building the Culture for Students with Severe Emotional-Behavioral Disabilities

Nancy Busse

I have often wondered why some students seem to enjoy finding out what they can get by with, but others behave in an entirely different manner. I have come to the conclusion that the students find no fun at all trying to disrupt learning environments in which they perceive their educators are making every effort to empower them, treat them as significant, and allow them to gain confidence in their ability to handle their own affairs. — Forrest Gathercoal, in *Judicious Discipline*

"*Judicious Discipline* will never work with students who have severe behavior problems." "Those students would never get the concepts or philosophy." "They would never buy into this." I have heard these sorts of statements over and over by colleagues throughout Minnesota and other states as I teach *Judicious Discipline* institutes. Yet, it is with "those students" that I first began using this approach. "They" do buy into this and find *Judicious Discipline* helpful to them in making good choices and being responsible school citizens.

Students with severe emotional/behavioral disabilities (EBD) are my passion. I have spent most of my teaching career working with this group of creative, high energy, stubborn, challenging students who have often given up on themselves.

I have been practicing the philosophy of *Judicious Discipline* for fourteen years and have worked as part of a team effectively

71

implementing *Judicious Discipline* in a secondary special education resource room setting for students with severe emotional/behavioral disabilities. I have also implemented it in two other sites, both of which were special education day treatment programs serving students kindergarten through twelfth grade with severe emotional/behavior disabilities and/or with significant mental health issues. How does anyone do that with "those" students?

Building a democratic culture starts with the language of rights and responsibilities. "Because every culture is grounded in its language, the first step is to learn something about our nation's democratic principles and how they can be integrated into the school environment" (Gathercoal, 2004, p. 51). The ten principles of *Judicious Discipline* are taught, as they are taught in any school environment. Discussions are held about student's rights, search and seizure, freedom of expression, physical health and safety, emotional health and safety, taking care of property, how to avoid disruptions, and being a responsible learner. Students make posters to help them apply *Judicious Discipline* in various environments around the school. Then the language is used as part of daily school life.

Judicious Discipline is a cognitive and intrinsic model. It is not designed to stand on its own, but to be used in conjunction with other cognitive resources. Behavior modification, level systems, and rewards and punishments are not used with this model. Skills are taught using curriculums such as Goldstein's "Skillstreaming," Vernon's "Thinking, Feeling, Behaving," Shure's "I Can Problem Solve," to name a few, to teach students new social skills, problem solving skills, how to recognize feelings, and learn new coping skills.

Students incorporate the cognitive, the behavioral skills taught, and practice these along with their rights and responsibilities to create an authentic learning and therapeutic environment in which they are active partners. They attend and frequently lead their progress review meetings which are held every seven weeks. Students have input into their programs, are part of the process, know what their goals are, and are part of keeping track of their daily progress data.

Judicious Discipline makes sense to students with emotional/behavioral disabilities because it is not some "made up" system. These are not arbitrary rules or a system that changes on a whim. These are the rights and expectations of our country based on the United States Constitution. Tangibles are not given or taken away. Students are treated respectfully. They have a job to do at school. They have rights and responsibilities to themselves, each other, and to the school community.

Using the concepts of *Judicious Discipline* means treating students fairly. In other words, each person gets what s/he needs for the best individualization of academic and behavior interventions. Each student's needs can be met in unique ways. This is no "cookie cutter" approach. No one size fits all. *Judicious Discipline* does not include punishment or pushing students out of school. Problem solving approaches are applied to all situations to decide what is going to work best for each student in each situation to come up with interventions that are effective and appropriate.

Whether interventions are needed for an academic situation or for a situation where a student has made a significant error in judgment, the approach is the same. What needs to be done now? What needs to be learned? What is going to help the student in this situation? Where do we go from here? Are there skills that need to be retaught? Are there skills that need to be practiced? Is there something in the environment that needs to be changed? Is there something that the staff needs to do differently? How can we make things better so that it doesn't happen again?

As the culture is established, the fun begins. Students with severe behavioral/emotional/mental health issues use their rights and responsibilities to test boundaries. Learning opportunities come in many ways. Let me share some examples. As new students joined the classroom, one female peer would always smile and say, "Has she read you your rights yet?"

As the Coordinator (administrator) of the Day Treatment Program, I had confiscated a senior high student's cell phone. I told him that I would not be able to give him a receipt for it, but I would give it back to his foster family. The student came to school the next day and reported to his class that he had read

73

through the student handbook the previous evening and there was nothing in the student handbook in regard to cell phones and he was quite sure that his cell phone needed to be returned to him. There was discussion in the classroom about how he should approach me with this issue. When should he talk to me? What tone of voice? What should he say? Basically, they were coaching him on reasonable time, place, and manner (TPM). I was unaware of any of this.

The student made an appointment, came to my office and told me that he wanted to use his due process. He stated that he had read through the student handbook and that there was no mention in it about students having cell phones in school and that he thought he should get his cell phone back. I said that he was correct. There was no mention of cell phones in the handbook. Then looking up at the bulletin board on the wall with the scale with the Rights and Responsibilities on it, I asked him which Responsibilities might be a concern with students having cell phones in school. "Disruption of the Educational Process," he said. "If the cell phone rang in class it would cause a disruption." "Yes," I agreed. "Anything else?" "Perhaps Health and Safety," he added. "How would that be?" I asked. "If the phone was being used to make drug deals," he stated very matter-of-factly. "Ah," I said, "that would certainly be Health and Safety." In fact, this was exactly my concern.

"What are you proposing?" I asked him. "I would like to take the cell phone home and I will not bring it back to school," he replied. "When would you get the cell phone?" "I could pick it up at the end of the day." "I can live with that. I will call your foster parents and see if that is OK with them," I stated. I called his foster parents who agreed with this arrangement. The student went back to his classroom with a swagger in his step and a smug look on his face as he reported to his peers that he had successfully used his due process and was getting his cell phone back at the end of the school day.

Another time the same student came to use his due process again. "I have a concern about my teacher. She is making me do more math and harder math than the other kids," he said. "Did you ask her about that?" I said. "Yes," he said, "She told me that I am very good at math and that I needed more of a challenge." "Is that accurate?" "Yes, I am good at math." "I would have to agree," I said, "I have read through your paperwork and your test scores are quite high in math. Did your teacher say anything else?" "She also said that she thought I was being a bit lazy when it came to math and that I ought to push myself." "Oh, what about that?" I queried. He chuckled a little and said, "Yeah, I don't want to work too hard. Math is harder for some of the other kids than it is for me." Looking up at the scale with the Rights and Responsibilities on it I said, "So you are telling me that your teacher has a Legitimate Educational Purpose for wanting you to do math that is at your level and that challenges you." The student looked at the scale and looked at me. "Never mind. I guess I'll go back to my class now." "OK. If you have any other concerns, I'd like to hear them," I said as he walked away.

In another situation, one severely EBD student was doing his school work and another EBD student was not. Instead of doing his assigned work, this student was being disruptive, trying to avoid his work, and get others off-task too. The other student looked at him and said, "You are disrupting my educational process. Please stop." The student looked at the other student, then stopped and began to do his school work. Both students were now on task. Sometimes it is just that simple when students know the language.

A group of Day Treatment senior high EBD students was having difficulty with disruptive behaviors during transportation. This concern was brought to me by the driver of their van. She talked about an issue over a cigarette lighter and how the students had then "ganged up" on her verbally over the issue. I said that I would talk with the students about the issue and get back to her after we had done some problem solving. The students start the day with a small group sharing session. Students share their feelings and set an individual goal for the day. The structure of the gathering is similar to a class meeting. I asked if I could join and bring up a concern at the end. The students agreed, giving each other a knowing look.

When it was the appropriate time, I said that there was a behavior concern during transportation on the way home the previous day. I asked if anyone would share what happened. One of the students said that she had been accused of having a cigarette lighter by the bus driver. Then the five students had joined in giving the driver a difficult time. I said, "As creative and funny as you all are, it would have been easy to play off of each other's comments and keep going and it would have been difficult to stop once you got started. I bet you gave her a tough time even though you knew it was the wrong thing to do." The students smiled, nodded, and gazed down. It is easy to imagine them getting carried away in a negative manner and verbally harassing the driver. "What needs to happen now?" I asked. One student volunteered, "We probably should apologize." "But she shouldn't accuse us of stuff," another student added. "How would you like to be reminded when your behavior starts to get out of line during transportation?" I inquired. "Could she give us a TPM (time, place, manner) reminder like we get here?" one student asked. "Would you all be willing to respond to a TPM reminder?" All of the students agreed that they would.

I arranged for the driver to meet with the students and myself at the end of the day. The students apologized and shared the plan. I also wrote a letter home to the parents explaining the problem and the solution the students had decided upon. The students further followed up on their plan by self-monitoring their behavior and setting behavior goals for transportation during morning check in at Day Treatment. A couple of weeks later a follow-up meeting was held with the driver. Everyone reported that things were going well. The driver reported that she had used a TPM reminder a couple of times and the students had immediately responded. I also wrote a follow-up letter to the parents informing them of the progress.

Students have taken the language with them as they make gains and return to their home schools and less restrictive environments. One Day Treatment student who was returning full time to her high school held a mini-inservice for her teachers to share what she needed. This student had been very disruptive to the high school environment in the past and not everyone was happy to see her return to the high school. The student used notecards for herself as she presented to her special education and regular education teachers, school counselor, school social worker, and assistant principal what her former behavior challenges/issues had been and what assistance she would need from them to help her continue using her knew coping skills and not falling back into old behavior patterns. One thing she needed was for her teachers to say TPM to her if she started becoming too boisterous, was not respecting personal boundaries, or was becoming too dramatic in class. All the teachers would need to say to her was, "TPM." This was new language to most of these folks. I passed out a copy of a letter that I had sent to parents, special education teachers, and assistant principals earlier in the school year explaining about reasonable Time, Place, and Manner (TPM). On the back of the letter was a copy of a TPM poster that is used at Day Treatment as a visual prompt. Imagine how impressed this group of professionals was with this student's ability to articulate her needs and interventions that would work for her.

There are numerous stories of power struggles being avoided when students have needed to be searched, of peers being able to respectfully express their health and safety concerns to each other when someone has lost control of their physical or verbal behavior, of students giving reminders to each other about their responsibilities, and of students using their due process to get their needs met rather than acting out. I have shared a few stories of the affect of a culture deliberately built on mutual respect and the principles of *Judicious Discipline*.

Judicious Discipline provides a framework for a student-centered approach building a culture of civility where "students will gain confidence and come to believe that educators will always be acting in their best interests" (Gathercoal, 2004, p. 28). It also provides a culture where students have self-efficacy. Their opinions, their ideas, *they* matter. The students are an important part of everything that happens. Yes, *Judicious Discipline* is very effective with "those" students who have very challenging behaviors and emotional problems.

References

Gathercoal, F. (2004). *Judicious Discipline*, 6th Ed. San Francisco: Caddo Gap Press.

Goldstein, A., & McGinnis, E. (2005). *Skillstreaming*. Champaign, IL: Research Press.

Shure, M. B. (2005). *I can problem solve*. Champaign, IL: Research Press.

Vernon, A. (2006). *Thinking, feeling, behaving*. Champaign, IL: Research Press.

Using Consequences Judiciously

Barbara Landau

When you have put into place and consistently used *Judicious Discipline* concepts—such as class meetings; Time, Place and Manner reminders; encouragement; and other preventive strategies for maintaining a peaceful learning environment—you will still come, at some point and with some students, to an inevitable need to use a consequence for an inappropriate behavior. The misconception about *Judicious Discipline* is that somehow ensuring the rights of students means never giving a consequence. That is not the case. The issue is what kind of consequence to use, and that decision is always informed by what you want to accomplish when you do use one.

When using consequences it is a mistake to restrict possible solutions to a small list of predetermined options that may or may not fit the problem that needs to be addressed. Students should be told at the beginning of the year that learning to maintain a safe school environment is like learning math or reading. Every student may need to receive slightly different information about what is expected, or receive the same information but in a different format. Teachers can assure students that management problems always will be addressed, but that not all students will receive the information in exactly the same way. As Forrest Gathercoal says "Treating everyone equally does not mean treating everyone the same."

79

The primary goal of a consequence should be restitution rather than shame. Some form of community service can be a very effective tool for having students learn to restore what they harmed or make amends for a misdeed. Teachers and students can work together at the beginning of the year to brainstorm some possible community service options. Remember though that these are not punishments but genuine opportunities for students to correct an inappropriate action. To give an example, if a student writes on a desk, the student should clean the desk. That would be restitution. If a student writes on a desk and must stay after school to clean all the desks, that would be a punishment.

Unfortunately, in the heat of anger or frustration, punishment is more often used when it comes to school consequences. Educators send students home or to detention—either way students are removed from the problems they have created. While this might seem like justice, in fact, the result is to remove the responsibility for actions from the students and shift the burden elsewhere. If students make messes, students are suspended. And who cleans up those messes? An alternative approach is to expect that students at least participate in putting things back the way they were, even if their participation consists of handing tools or cleaning solutions to an adult.

Sometimes restitution may not be appropriate or may not be the first response. There are other options and the more the better. Other possible consequences might include:

* *Conference with teacher and parents.* Parents should be partners in this as they are in all aspects of their student's education. Too often students hear the threat "If you do that again, I will call your parents." Pitting families against schools makes little sense pedagogically. Parents can and should be included in management decisions as they are in other educational decisions.

* *A sincere apology.* Remember, as with other consequences, the apology should be developed with the student's participation. A mumbled "I'm sorry" in response to an adult's command to apologize can hardly be considered sincere.

* *Redoing an assignment.* The dog may well have eaten the homework. That really is not the issue. More pertinent in this situation is the teacher's need to assess the student's work. That assessment cannot occur if the homework resides in the dog's digestive track, in a forgotten book or nowhere at all. Whatever the excuse, the student does not need a lecture on the validity of the excuse. The student needs to be asked: "When can I expect your work so I can assess it and we can both learn more about your educational needs.?"

* *Time Out.* Taking time to cool down and gather one's thoughts is an important anger management skill. Educators can help students learn how to do this by saying something like: "You seem pretty upset right now. I'm wondering if you would like some time out to collect yourself. Then, when you've cooled down, we can try talking again." This should be said in a very positive tone. We are trying to get students to assess their own levels of anger and handle the emotions in ways that do not hurt themselves or others.

However, students need some help with what time out is all about. I once saw a student who was instructed to take time out and get himself together. He walked into the hall, gave himself a brief shake, pivoted around, and walked back in. He was out of the room in "time out" for maybe five or six seconds. Perhaps something more is needed.

One teacher shared a unique idea for time out. He provides students with a corner that contains a comfortable chair, some ocean pictures, and a tape of soothing ocean sounds. Another teacher provides students with drawing and writing materials. The equipment used is not as important as the message that calming down takes a little time and a little work.

Students can be offered the opportunity to take time out or they can opt for it themselves. A student who announces "I think I need some time out right now,"

should be congratulated. There is some very good decision making happening with this statement. Certainly
students should not spend an entire day in a quiet corner,
but they should be able to take a reasonable amount of
time to recover.

Time out should never mean sitting in the hall. The
humiliation that accompanies this practice negates any
value the student might gain from a cooling down time.
There are also serious confidentiality issues involved.
Anyone walking down the hall sees who is sitting outside
the classroom door. It marks a student as a problem.
Finally, sitting a student alone in the hall is dangerous.
Far too many students view being placed in the hall as an
opportunity to leave school.

Loss of Privileges. On an occasional basis this can be an
effective practice. However, there are some events in a
school day that are not privileges but neither are they
academics. Recess, lunch, and field trips are as important
to a student's learning as are math and spelling lessons.
They should not be taken away arbitrarily or routinely.
Teachers may need some time to speak with a student.
When that need arises students can be asked what time
would be best for a conference. The options will likely
include lunch, recess, or after school. It is not necessary
to place an undo burden on teachers, but it is important
to realize that peer relationships and fresh air are vital
needs for everyone. Teachers should never view depriv-
ing students of those activities as something that can be
done routinely.

Problem Solving Rooms. In-school suspension can be a
useful way to provide a student with individual attention
when there are few other options. Remember the goal
here is not to punish but to help students recover and get
them back on track. One school staffs its in-school
suspension or problem-solving room with retired people
who are volunteering their time. Students who spend

time in this room receive help with their homework, work through some problem solving with the adult present, and consider ways that they can best repair their relationship with their teacher. Whatever plans are developed in the room are written down and three copies are made. One copy goes into the student's file to track behavior concerns, one copy goes back to the teacher, and one copy is mailed to the parents. This way, all the parties are informed who need to be.

* *Counseling.* A troubled student may need help that is far beyond the capabilities of the teacher to address. Educators should not hesitate to recruit other skilled personnel to assist us. Teachers can only do so much, and professional responsibilities dictate that problems be referred to those who have the time and resources to help students more.

Out-of-school resources are certainly an option. If the problem is something like substance abuse, the help for it may be found in the community. Diversion programs can be recommended to families before students become truly addicted or run afoul of the law. Parents must be the ones who decide how such a problem is handled. The role of educators is to spot the problem and see it for the concern it is. Diversion programs are typically established by law enforcement agencies. Suspending students from school while making no effort to share concerns with parents may not result in the student getting the needed help.

Peer Justice

In an attempt to develop a justice model for classroom management, some teachers have instituted the practice of having peers put peers on trial. Typically problems are handled in a mock trial type of setting during which individual student behaviors are discussed and judged by a panel of other students or by an entire class. The concern with such a practice is that students often act out in class because of very personal events occurring in their lives. Given all the private reasons that might be involved in a student's misbehavior, the search for solutions through peer trials is simply not appropriate. Peers have no need to know about the special needs and interests of other students. Teachers are the educational leaders in classrooms and it is imperative that they take the lead when determining the best way to help students recover from problems. Educators simply should not relinquish their professional responsibility to young people who have not had the life experience that leads to wisdom and moral reasoning.

Some Final Thoughts about Consequences

There is no magic formula for the perfect consequence. Teachers might not need to use them at all. But, if it is deemed to be an appropriate step to help students learn from their mistakes, then whatever actions are taken should reflect a creative and flexible attitude. Remember that the goal is to help students recover from their mistakes and acquire new skills they previously might not have had. Teachers should see the use of consequences as an opportunity to respond to problems in ways that best suit individual needs and preserve the safety of the larger learning community.

Finally, do all you can to keep it confidential. There is no need for a public display. Help students walk away from difficult situations with their dignity in place.

Conducting Democratic Class Meetings

Paul Gathercoal

It is at least difficult, if not impossible, to prepare students as responsible citizens in a free, democratic society by teaching about democracy in autocratic schools and classrooms. Students need democratic models operating in their daily lives and opportunities to exercise their democratic rights and responsibilities in schools and classrooms. They need educators who can model appropriate language, knowledge, and dispositions at a principled level of reasoning with concomitant management strategies; they need to learn as participatory citizens in democratic schools and classrooms (Hill, 1990; McEwan, 1990; Sarason, 1990; Glickman, Allen & Lunsford, 1994; Gathercoal, 1999; McEwan, Gathercoal & Nimmo, 1999; Landau & Gathercoal, 2000; Gathercoal & Nimmo, 2002). *Judicious Discipline* is the only model for school discipline and classroom management that is based on principles of democracy and that operates at the principled level of moral development (Wolfgang, 1995).

The ideas and strategies for conducting *democratic class meetings*, articulated in this chapter, emanate from and are informed by an action research project that studied the effect *Judicious Discipline* had on an elementary and middle school in southern Minnesota (Gathercoal & Nimmo, 2002). The results of the study suggested that when teachers use strategies complementary with the philosophy of *Judicious Discipline* they lead students toward the autonomous stage of social development, as measured by a social development questionnaire administered to students in their classroom groups (McEwan, Gathercoal, & Nimmo, 1999). The research indicates that students became more self-directed and that they were able to take responsibility for learning. They displayed flexibility in a variety of social situations without demanding conformity of all students. They were able to empathize with others and establish mutual expectations based on respect for themselves and others.

The action research project findings also suggested that teachers need to take class time to teach students about their individual rights and responsibilities. Teachers who take this class time reap many benefits:

· Their students are more likely to indicate that they are operational at the autonomous stage of social development on the social development questionnaires;

· They are less likely to feel frustrated and/or experience high levels of work-related stress;

· They are more likely to be respected by others;

· They will feel a sense of professionalism;

· They are using management strategies that are legal, ethical, and educationally sound;

· Their students learn to use a "language of civility," which offers a common ground for discussing, mediating and reconciling social problems; and

· Their students use this "language of civility" to advocate for themselves and to solve social problems.

The study also indicated that teachers who conducted *democratic class meetings* while implementing *Judicious Discipline* tended to benefit more, in terms of peaceful resolution to conflict and quality instructional time, than teachers who did not conduct *democratic class meetings*. This finding emerged in both the quantitative and qualitative data that was collected. As a result, the study recommends that implementation of *Judicious Discipline* works best when teachers concomitantly conduct *democratic class meetings*. The data identified certain key elements that helped *democratic class meetings* to run more smoothly when teachers included these key elements in their repertoire of teaching strategies and logistically conducted the class meeting with these key elements in mind. The purpose of this chapter is to share the key elements for conducting *democratic class meetings* that research supports as successful strategies.

Guidelines for Democratic Class Meetings

The elements for conducting *democratic class meetings* that follow were gleaned from interviews with students and teachers who found strategies that worked best for them when conducting *democratic class meetings*.

That being said, it seems extraordinary to start with this statement:

There is no "right way" to conduct a *democratic class meeting.*

The research indicated that successful *democratic class meetings* took many different forms and that the "best" organization and structure for any given class group will probably emerge as the academic year progresses. Nonetheless, some strategies and dispositions that work well to facilitate and democratize class meetings emerged from the research as "key elements" for success. The following is a list of key elements that will be helpful for teachers who are organizing and conducting *democratic class meetings* for the first time.

The Key Elements
for Conducting *Democratic Class Meetings*

· *Determine who can call a class meeting and when they*

should be held. (What is a reasonable time, place, and manner?) Some teachers allow any student in the class to call a class meeting whenever one is necessary. Other teachers determine a specific time, place, and manner. Both methods and a variety of methods in-between can work well as long as the calling of a class meeting has the effect of giving students a sense of significance and some power and control over what happens in their classroom. The important element is that *democratic class meetings* will occur and that there is some mechanism for calling a class meeting to order.

· *All students and the teacher should be seated so everyone can see the faces of the others in the class meeting.* How we position ourselves says much about power relationships. To instill a sense of significance and power in the students, *sit in a circle or square shape where everyone can communicate easily with any other person in the class meeting.* The physical environment in the classroom should be as *inclusive* as possible, and students and teachers who sit comfortably in a closed circle provide for a feeling of community that encourages positive and productive communication. The more "formal" physical arrangements (sitting in rows) have the effect of excluding students, or allowing students to exclude themselves. This feeling of exclusion may occur for other reasons, e.g., name-calling, or an individual's posture within the circle; but, by sitting in a circle, the physical environment is optimized and communication is amplified.

· *Set the ground rule / expectation that we will never use names during the class meetings.* Using names casts an accusatory finger at the person being named and has the effect of putting that person on the defense. It also causes ill feelings. Negotiate with students not to use class members' names. Ask, "How would you feel if everyone in the class was talking about you?" Most students would feel embarrassed and defensive. Suggest that when talking about problems and behaviors that the class should talk in terms of, "a person who acts in this way..." rather than, "When (Person's Name) acts like..." This protects individuals in the class and allows them to participate in the discussion about behaviors and ideas and not about personalities.

· *Set the ground rule / expectation that we will stay on the topic and carefully guard any sharing about our families during the class meetings.* The efficiency of any class meeting is mediated by the class' ability to stay on topic and to discuss all agenda items with an open mind. By guarding carefully what is brought to the attention of the meeting and by keeping the topic free of "family concerns" the class meeting is more likely to flow quickly and smoothly.

· *The teacher should lead the class meeting.* The research project indicated that when teachers hand over the leadership role to students, the class meeting digresses. Many teachers think having "Class Officers" and empowering them with the administrative power to lead the meeting is "in line" with democratic principles and that the practice leads students to autonomy. In fact, our research findings indicate the opposite. The whole process of deciding and empowering "Class Officers" propagates popularity contests, competition and a "privileged class." These contests generate ill feelings and can result in a major break down in community building. *There should be one educational leader in the classroom and that educational leader is the teacher.* The teacher needs to facilitate and conduct the *democratic class meeting.*

· *Students should never be coerced to participate in the class meeting.* It is a good idea to set the ground rule that it is okay to "pass" if an individual chooses not to contribute to the discussion.

· *It is a good idea for each student and the teacher to have a class meeting journal.* In this journal the teacher and students can record their thoughts. Kindergarten students can record their thoughts in a journal, too. Often, the younger students record their thoughts as pictures. This is okay; it is a powerful feeling when students view themselves as writers and readers and providing students with their own journal helps them to feel ownership in the class discussion.

· *A good way to begin class meetings is to write in your journal for a few minutes.* This writing can occur at the beginning of class or at the end of class, and it can take place in small groups or be done individually. It is a good idea to vary the format, write in small groups for one meeting, and individually for the next meeting.

· *It is important that the teacher participates by writing in his or her journal.* This sends a strong message to the students that this is important work; so important that the students' writing will be valued along with the teacher's writing.

· *Give guidelines or categories for writing in the journals and display these guidelines for all to see.* You may want to change the guidelines or categories from meeting to meeting. Some guidelines or categories that have worked well are: Concerns, Clarifications, and Delights, *or* Something I'd Like To Talk About, Something I'd Like To Work On, and Things That Are Going Well. Using three categories and encouraging everyone to write at least one thing in each category is a good idea. Ensure that one of the categories allows students to raise issues that are problem areas, another category will allow for their questions, and the third category encourages celebrations and the acknowledgment of success.

· *After everyone has had time to write in their journal, assemble in a circle and use the journal entries as the agenda for the democratic class meeting.* Begin by asking, "Does anyone have concerns or clarifications they would like to discuss?" Save the "Delights" for the end of the meeting; "Delights" and things that are going well tend to make everyone feel good and sharing our successes does much to build community amongst the class group.

· *It is a good idea for the students and the teacher to set and write down goals.* The teacher and students can use their class meeting journal to write down goals that they set for themselves. It is important that individuals set their own goals; no one should ever set a goal for someone else. It's okay to suggest possible goals as questions, "What do you think about setting a goal like, ...?" But, never dictate a goal for someone else. This can only bring about a co-dependent relationship and destroy a viable mentoring relationship.

· *Writing goals down is important.* Verbalizing goals and writing them down in a journal accomplishes several things. It gives us something to strive for that is in a form we can visualize. It encourages us to take ownership in problem-solving; and it gives us a measuring stick for our personal growth and performance in life. Writing the goal down is important, but sharing the goal with others is another matter.

· *Never direct members of the class to share their goals with others.* If students choose to share their goal, that is fine, but some goals are more personal than others, and it is not for anyone else to decide what is personal and what is not. For example, one student may write down the goal, "I need to start listening better." When teachers direct students to share a goal with others, students run the risk of being mocked and taunted with, "You need to listen better!" and this can cause ill feelings and it will not help the student to make an honest self-assessment of his or her progress or encourage him or her to set more goals in the future. In fact, teachers may want to warn their students, "It's important to write your goals down (and cite the reasons above as to why it is important), but be careful who you share your goals with and be sure and celebrate when you accomplish the goals you set for yourself."

· *Self-assess the goals individuals have set for themselves.* The teacher can ask, "How are we going with the goals we set last meeting?" Without iterating the goal, the teacher and students can report, "I'm doing pretty good" or "I'm having some trouble with my goal." This allows the class to celebrate with those who achieve their goals and offer moral support for those who may not be achieving as much as they think they should. Note that at no time does the person have to state what the goal is, they just offer an assessment of their progress. As with other agenda items, the teacher and student should all have the right to "pass" if they do not wish to respond to this question.

The Action Research Project

Students and educators in two schools in Southwest Minnesota participated in the research. One school was an Elementary School with approximately 425 students in grades one through five, and the other was a Middle School with approximately 300 sixth grade students. Quantitative data was collected through a questionnaire administered to all students in both schools three times throughout the 1995-96 school year. Qualitative data was collected through videotaped interviews with educators and students.

During the month of September, students at both schools were taught about *Judicious Discipline*. Instruction began with presentations by the school principal, counselor, and other resource staff, e.g., school psychologists and police liaison officer. After these initial presentations, classroom teachers taught lessons about rights and responsibilities, including the concept of appropriate "time, place, and manner." Lesson plans were made available to every classroom teacher; however, it was left to the classroom teacher's discretion as to the amount of time used for these lessons and the amount of follow-up that occurred after the initial presentations.

Throughout the year, various interventions by resource staff occurred in both schools in order that the faculty and staff be made aware of the principles embedded in *Judicious Discipline* and the successful strategies that were being used to implement it in the classroom. As well, faculty, administration, and staff held meetings for the purpose of brainstorming democratic methods and individual strategies for dealing with student behavior. At the Elementary School, a *Judicious Discipline* empowerment group, of interested faculty, administration and staff, met regularly to discuss delights and concerns with its implementation. At the Middle School, discussions occurred on an as needed basis to brainstorm "judicious" responses to specific student behaviors.

Through these discussions, strategies and ideas were developed with teachers who wanted to deal with particular behavior problems, specific to their classroom. Discussions of this nature occurred when teachers indicated that certain students could have affected the results of their class group's social development responses. The discussion then centered on how the teachers might deal with the behavior problem "judiciously" in their classroom setting, either through *democratic class meetings* or through private discussions with the students.

The Importance of Democratic Class Meetings

Democratic class meetings provide students with a sense of value and belonging. They are an essential part of the effective operation of *all Judicious Discipline* classrooms. *Democratic class meetings* are needed at all levels of education, as these meetings provide excellent opportunities for developing and discussing goals, expectations, and relationships within the educational setting.

Democratic class meetings work to share power; and as a result, they do much to *avoid power struggles* by providing every student with an opportunity to express concerns, questions, and delights. When students feel that they have some power in the organization and operation of their class, they are less likely to "act out." Class meetings provide "institutionally okay" ways for students to vent their frustrations and anxieties; and to celebrate in a fair and equitable manner. When decisions are made in the class meeting, and if there is action to be taken, *students are more likely to participate* because they feel like they are an important part of the decision-making process. *Democratic class meetings* are opportunities for *teachers to model respect and trust* by actively listening to and valuing their students' ideas.

Over a two-year period of time, it became evident that conducting *democratic class meetings* had a significant effect on the implementation of *Judicious Discipline* in classroom settings. The significant effect *democratic class meetings* had on implementation manifest itself both years through quantitative analysis of student responses on their social development questionnaires and videotaped interviews with students and educators.

The social development questionnaire was developed by *The Social Development Group*, Research Branch of the South Australian Department of Education, and published in their 1980 publication *Developing the Classroom Group*. It differentiates between power and affect relationships through a series of eight true/false questions and places individual student responses in one of four developmental stages (dependent, rebellion, cohesion, and autonomy).

Student behavior for each stage of social development is described below:

· In *stage 1*, the main issue is dependence. Students are generally dependent and submissive, and do what the teacher says. The students' interaction is mostly through the teacher, so there is low covert interaction among students. There is little disruptive behavior, but some "attention getting." Order is fairly high. Anxiety levels are high in some students. Some students are bored. Motivation is extrinsic; approval, praise and encouragement from the teacher and parent/caregiver(s) is important. There is fear of punishment.

· In *stage 2* the main issue is rebellion. The students test, challenge and try out the teacher. The student group separates into two camps, one in opposition to the teacher, the other seeking to maintain dependent group behavior. Some students challenge or ignore the teacher's efforts to control the class. Noise level tends to be high. Trust levels among students are low, and aggressive interactions and put downs are common. The rebellious sub-group is extrinsically motivated by peer group approval, moderated by fear of teacher punishment. The intrinsic motivation is for autonomy, moderated by dependency needs.

· In *stage 3*, the main issue is cohesion. Students are friendly and trusting to each other and the teacher. There is very little disruptive behavior. There is a lot of interaction but of an orderly type. They conform to group norms. There is little disagreement, as this is seen as disruptive to the harmony of the group. This inability to handle conflict results in some covert bad feelings. Extrinsic motivation comes from praise and encouragement from peer group and teacher. Breach of class norms brings strong group disapproval.

· Autonomy is the main issue at *stage 4*. Individuals are self-directed, able to seek and give support but function well without it. Students take responsibility for their own learning. There is a high level of interaction. Agreement and discussion are the norm; agreement occurs in the context of disagreement.

Feelings (positive and negative) are openly expressed. Students work the same with or without the teacher present.

Disruptive behavior is virtually non-existent. Students show flexibility and adaptability in a variety of learning situations without demanding conformity of all members. They utilize self-awareness and empathy rather than rules to choose behavior. Motivation is mainly intrinsic. Social behavior is based on respect for self and others. Learning is seen as a way of gaining personal competence and joy. (Education Department of South Australia, 1980, p. 31-35)

The sixth-grade-only school involved in the research project, housed approximately 300 students in twelve distinct home rooms. Two home room teachers conducted *democratic class meetings* throughout the first year of the study and ten home room teachers did not. A comparison of social development questionnaire results for each home room indicates that the two teachers who conducted *democratic class meetings* generated a class climate that was more aligned with the autonomous stage of social development than did the ten teachers who did not conduct *democratic class meetings*.

At the beginning of the year, the two teachers who conducted *democratic class meetings* had similar results to teachers who did not conduct *democratic class meetings*. This indicates that the classes were probably similar in their stages of social development at the beginning of the year.

The results of social development questionnaires administered at the beginning of the academic year for teachers who conducted *democratic class meetings* and those who did not conduct *democratic class meetings* are presented in Table 1. The reported "N" indicates the number of responses that were given

Table1.
Results of Student Responses to Questionnaires in September.

Teachers Who Conducted *Democratic Class Meetings*
September 1995 Questionnaire Results

Dependent	Rebellion	Cohesive	Autonomous
N = 76: 49%	N = 20: 13%	N = 54: 26%	N = 54: 26%

Teachers Who Did Not Conduct *Democratic Class Meetings*
September 1995 Questionnaire Results

Dependent	Rebellion	Cohesive	Autonomous
N = 412: 40%	N = 145: 14%	N = 248: 24%	N = 223: 22%

by all students who responded on the questionnaire at a particular stage of social development for four constructs (teacher power, student power, student/student relationship, and teacher/student relationship). While the "N" for each group is different, the percentages of respondents at any given stage of social development are probably equal.

By February 1996, differences in survey results began to emerge and qualitative data indicated that students who were involved in *democratic class meetings* felt more empowered and felt more of a sense of belonging to the class group. The February results indicated that while the school was making good progress in the area of social development, the two teachers who conducted *democratic class meetings* made great progress.

The social development questionnaire results for teachers who conducted *democratic class meetings* and those who did not conduct *democratic class meetings* in February 1996 are presented in Table 2. Again, the reported "N" indicates the number of responses that were given by all students answering at a particular stage of social development for the four constructs (teacher power, student power, student/student relationship, and teacher/student relationship) and while the "N" for each group is different, the percentages of respondents at any given stage of social development are probably not equal.

The May social development questionnaire results continue

Table 2.
Results of Student Responses to Questionnaires in February.

Teachers Who Conducted *Democratic Class Meetings*
February 1996 Questionnaire Results

Dependent	Rebellion	Cohesive	Autonomous
N = 11: 6%	N = 19: 10%	N = 18: 9%	N = 148: 76%

Teachers Who Did Not Conduct *Democratic Class Meetings*
February 1996 Questionnaire Results

Dependent	Rebellion	Cohesive	Autonomous
N = 170: 17%	N = 224: 23%	N = 193: 20%	N = 399: 40%

to show that the two teachers who conducted *democratic class meetings* maintained a high response rate for students' reporting that they were operating at the autonomous stage of social development and the ten teachers who *did not* conduct *democratic class meetings* tended to have their students respond very high on social development questionnaire at the rebellion stage.

The questionnaire results for teachers who conducted *democratic class meetings* and those who did not conduct *democratic class meetings* in May 1996 are presented in Table 3. The reported "N" indicates the number of responses that were given by all students answering at a particular stage of social development for the four constructs (teacher power, student power, student/student relationship, and teacher/student relationship) and while the "N" for each group is different, the percentages of respondents at any given stage of social development are again, probably not equal.

These results support the need for conducting *democratic class meetings* when implementing *Judicious Discipline*.

Educators may be well advised to include *democratic class meetings* in their repertoire of teaching strategies when they implement the principles of *Judicious Discipline* in their classrooms and schools. As educators shift from autocratic class management practices to a more democratic style of administration, it serves educators and their students well to have the key

Table 3.
Results of Student Responses to Questionnaires in May.

Teachers Who Conducted *Democratic Class Meetings*
May 1996 Questionnaire Results

Dependent	Rebellion	Cohesive	Autonomous
N = 11: 6%	N = 11: 6%	N = 28: 14%	N = 150: 75%

Teachers Who Did Not Conduct *Democratic Class Meetings*
May 1996 Questionnaire Results

Dependent	Rebellion	Cohesive	Autonomous
N = 158: 16%	N = 268: 27%	N = 182: 18%	N = 383: 37%

elements for conducting *democratic class meetings* in place. When *democratic class meetings* are conducted in concert with the practice of *Judicious Discipline*, educators can feel good about their teaching and know that they are truly helping to prepare tomorrow's citizens for living and learning in a democratic, free society.

References

Education Department of South Australia (1980). *Developing the classroom group: A manual for the inservice trainer*. Report No. 4. Adelaide, South Australia: Government Printer of South Australia.

Gathercoal, F. (2004). *Judicious discipline*, 6th Ed. San Francisco: Caddo Gap Press.

Gathercoal, P. (2004). How action research has informed the practice of judicious discipline. In F. Gathercoal, *Judicious Discipline* (6th Ed.). San Francisco: Caddo Gap Press.

Gathercoal, P., & Nimmo, V. (2002). Judicious discipline: Democracy in education. *Journal of Thought* (Summer), 73-88.

Gathercoal, P. (1999). Judicious discipline and neuroscience: Constructing a neurological rationale for democracy in the classroom. In B.M. Landau (Ed.), *Practicing judicious discipline: An educator's guide to a democratic classroom*, 3rd Ed. San Francisco: Caddo Gap Press.

Gathercoal, P., & Connolly, J. (Producers). (1997). *Conducting democratic class meetings* [Video]. Available from Corroboree, LLC., 159 Glenbrook Avenue, Camarillo, CA 93010.

Glickman, C., Allen, L., & Lunsford, B. (1994). Voices of principals from democratically transformed schools. In J. Murphy & K. Louis (Eds.). *Reshaping the principalship: Insights from transformational reform efforts*. Thousand Oaks, CA: Corwin Press.

Hill, D. (April, 1990). Order in the classroom. *Teacher*, 70-77.

Kohlberg, L. (1976). Moral stages and moralization: The cognitive-developmental approach. In T. Lickora (Ed.), *Moral development and behavior*. New York: Holt, Rinehart, & Winston.

Landau, B., & Gathercoal, P. (2000). Creating peaceful classrooms: *Judicious discipline and class meetings. Phi Delta Kappan, 81*(6), 450-454.

McEwan, B. (1990). Review. Judicious discipline. *Democracy and Education, 4*(3), 37-40.

McEwan, B., Gathercoal, P., & Nimmo, V. (1999). Application of judicious discipline: A common language for classroom management. In H. J. Freiberg (Ed.), *Beyond behaviorism: Changing the classroom management paradigm*. Boston: Allyn & Bacon.

Murphy, J., & Louis, K. (1995). *Reshaping the Principalship: Insights from transformational reform efforts*. Thousand Oaks, CA: Corwin Press.

Sarason, S. (1990). *The predictable failure of educational reform*. San Francisco: Jossey-Bass.

Wolfgang, C. (1995). *Solving discipline problems: Methods and models for today's teachers*. Boston: Allyn & Bacon.

The ABCs
of Democratic Classroom
Management

Julie Petersen

A. Acknowledge, Accept, and Respect
Students As Citizens

Perhaps one of the greatest underlying theses of the *Judicious Discipline* philosophy is the need to first *Acknowledge, Accept and Respect Students* as permanently valued citizens who have rights and responsibilities within the learning community.

B. Belonging, Believing, and Becoming

The unfolding development of a child within the judicious classroom is evident in their equal opportunity for an education which will enable them to *belong* to a group, *believe* in their individual rights and responsibilities, and *become* valued citizens within the classroom and our nation's society.

C. Compelling State Interests

There are four *Compelling State Interests* on which the basic student responsibilities are based. These interests include Health and Safety, Property Loss and Damage, Serious Disruption of the Educational Process, and Legitimate Educational Purpose.

D. Democratic Approach to Discipline with Dignity

A judicious classroom is one that is truly democratic and student centered in its approach to building self-esteem and empowering all learning experiences to include discipline with dignity.

E. Equality within the Educational Environment

One of the many strengths of *Judicious Discipline* can be found in the guiding principle, taken from the Fourteenth Amendment, which assures every child the right to an equal opportunity for an education.

F. Freedom

Another guiding principle, taken from the First Amendment, assures every child *freedom*.

G. Gathering in Groups Together

Working cooperatively is a natural part of a democratic classrooms. Children *gathering in groups together* have an opportunity to learn from each other and appreciate the unique attributes of each group member.

H. Honesty

One of the essential components of the philosophy also requires teachers and students to practice *honesty* and to be accountable at all times.

I. Individual Differences

One cannot think of an educational approach to discipline that is as empowering or respectful of student *individual differences*.

J. Justice

One of the guiding principles of our democracy is to ensure all students the *justice* of due process.

K. Knowledge

We gather together in a learning community to acquire *knowledge*. The respect we show each other and the responsibilities we assume all support our mutual quest for knowledge.

L. Language

The judicious philosophy is enhanced by its empowering and democratic *language*. Students will be encouraged to establish a specific vocabulary which addresses their individual rights and responsibilities as well as those same liberties of others.

M. Manner

When a child is struggling with meeting the responsibilities of his or her rights, it is important to ask the child "Is this the appropriate *manner* in which to....?"

N. Needs

A judicious plan for discipline acknowledges that with every right a student is given comes a responsibility. The suggested guidelines for responsible behaviors are based on the four welfare *needs* of the state.

O. Opportunities to Succeed

The judicious classroom assures opportunities for student success academically, behaviorally, emotionally, and physically. All students are invited in to a safe and secure learning environment which values them and their right to learn.

P. Place

If a student is struggling with how to make an appropriate choice, ask "Is this the appropriate *place* in which to....?"

Q. Questions

Asking *questions* as a means of redirection is a very effective strategy. When students are asked "What happened?" or "How may I help you?" they are empowered to consider their own choices for behavior.They are cooperatively involved with the teacher in making a decision and solving the problem at hand.

R. Rights and Responsibilities

Students learn valuable life lessons about the *rights* they are ensured under the Constitution, the *responsibilities* that accompany these rights, and the judicious consequences that follow an infraction upon these rights.

S. Student Centered Supportive Learning Environment

The judicious approach to discipline is designed to create and support a *student centered supportive learning environment.*

T. Time

When a student is considering a choice about appropriate behavior, ask "Is this the appropriate *time* in which to.....?" Asking students to consider the appropriate *time, place,* and *manner* for behaviors helps them make responsible decisions.

U. United States Constitution

Democratic management reflects the democratic principles of the *United States Constitution* applied to classroom management. Students become permanently valued citizens in their classrooms today and contributing members of society tomorrow.

V. Value

One of the most important aspects of this philosophy is its recognition of individual *value* and worth within the learning community.

W. Win-Win Experiences

Judicious management ensures a teacher and student will experience *win-win* outcomes to their cooperative decision making without power struggles.

X. Xenophobia

Classrooms focused on mutual success, respect, and responsibility reduce *xenophobic* attitudes towards students from diverse cultural backgrounds.

Y. You

As a classroom teacher, *you* encourage or discourage students from learning; you invite their success or their failure based on your preparation and presentation of the concepts addressed.

Z. Zero Tolerance

There is no place for *zero tolerance* within a democratic classroom because the consequences to correct behaviors are designed to be educational in nature rather than embarrassing, humiliating, or punishing. While there are words and actions that can hurt a classroom environment, an educator's response must be informative. We can not teach tolerance while modeling intolerance.

Tips for Putting
Judicious Discipline
into Your Classroom

Barbara Landau
(Originally Developed in Cooperation with Margaret Abbott)

Any management framework that emphasizes the value of building equitable, nurturing relationships with and among students takes time and effort. There is no "cookbook" for such an approach, nor should there be. Human relationships are exciting, dynamic and interesting because of their complexity.

On the other hand, it's always nice to have some basic "how-to" ideas that will help you get started using Judicious Discipline. It is in that spirit that I offer the following ideas.

1. Prepare lesson plans for introducing your students to their individual rights, the compelling state interests, and the balance between the two. If you are introducing these ideas in the middle of the year, point out to students how the existing classroom rules you have been using are already aligned with the compelling state interests, or how they might easily be reworked to reflect those interests. If you are implementing *Judicious Discipline* at the beginning of the year you are invited to use any of the several lesson plans contained in this book, adapt any of the lessons or create some of your own.

2. As you consider ways to make your classroom a more

equitable learning environment, do not forget to look at your room arrangement. Can all the areas of your room be easily accessed? Could a student in a wheel chair easily move through and around your classroom? Is the classroom visually appealing? Can students easily access materials they might need during the day? Can you move around easily so that you are not confined to the front of the room? Answering these questions will be a good start toward creating a physical environment that is considerate of all your students.

3. As you guide your students through the process of creating classroom rules, make sure they are rules you can live with. A rule prohibiting eating or drinking in the classroom won't work for you if you are accustomed to sipping coffee while you teach. Similarly, if you are a teacher who pats students on the shoulder as a congratulatory gesture, a rule stating "Keep hands and feet to yourself" will have you modeling that it is ok to break rules when you want to.

4. Once you have developed the rules, check to make sure your students understand the rules. The lesson plans in Section Two have a lot of ideas for checking such as drawing pictures, role playing, revisiting the rules during morning meetings. However you do it, remember that developing the rules is only the first step. Revisiting them and making sure students understand them will help make your classroom a safe and productive learning environment.

5. *Judicious Discipline* strongly encourages open communication with parents. Primary caregivers should be partners in the education of their students and teachers using *Judicious Discipline* do all they can to invite parents and other responsible adults into the process. Many teachers have websites parents can visit on line to check on assignments, classroom activities, etc. If you

have a website, this is an ideal place to post information on *Judicious Discipline* and how you will be implementing it in your classroom.

Knowing that all families do not have access to technology in their homes, you should also prepare a letter to send to each student's primary care giver. The website and the letter explain the new policies in your classroom and your rationale for using *Judicious Discipline* as a decision-making framework. Translate or have translated the information into all the languages spoken in each child's home or place of primary care.

6. Design a poster that will inform students of your professional ethics. Consider it the equivalent of your personal *Hippocratic Oath*. You might want to review the NEA Statement of Professional Ethics for some ideas and language.

Discuss your ethical beliefs briefly with your students, and then ask them to develop a set of classroom ethics. Post their statement of ethics next to your own.

7. *Judicious Discipline* works best when it is supported by on-going class meetings. Class meetings offer you the opportunity to revisit rules and expectations on a regularly scheduled basis and provide students a chance to voice concerns or questions in an open and accepting environment. In the first section of this book, there is an article explaining the merits of class meetings and how to implement them.

8. Keep a basket of in-class assignments. If your students are absent, tell them that the work they missed can be found in the designated baskets. This helps them to become personally responsible for the work they do.

9. Avoid the classic path to power struggles—assessment. First and foremost, students need to know what is

expected of them and what they need to do in order to be successful. Grading matrices or scoring rubrics –their names are unimportant—but providing students with grids that delineate the graded elements of an assignment and what an outstanding, acceptable, or needs improvement assignment would look like eases everyone's stress level. Once students are familiar with scoring rubrics, have them begin to develop their own. When expectations are clear and fair, power struggles diminish.

10. Let students know how you will address late or missing work. Explain that they will receive an Incomplete until their work is handed in. Make it clear that you will not grade work down if an assignment is late, nor will you assign an "F" to it if it is not handed in. When you consider all the reasons why assignments might be late or missing, it is important to value the equal opportunity for all students to be successful over an arbitrary deadline.

Hold a class meeting to discuss the importance of each assignment. Explain to your students that all the work they do has a Legitimate Educational Purpose and must be completed in order for you to assess their progress in class.

11. Set up a system of two baskets in your classroom, one for late papers and one for papers in on time. Explain to your students that the papers in on time will be graded promptly and returned, but the papers submitted to the late basket will be graded when you are able to do them. Papers in the late basket may result in the student receiving an Incomplete.

12. If you need to speak with a student about a problem, whisper to the student, find a quiet corner, or step into the hallway so that your conversation can preserve the confidentiality to which the student is entitled.

The right to confidentiality also protects the students

from having their names put on public display when they have misbehaved. This means no names on the board, no turning cards with students names on them or moving clothes pins with students names on them. Singling out students in any of those ways only widens the communication gap between you and the students you are responsible for.

Protecting confidentiality also includes what you say or do not say in the presence of your colleagues. Student behaviors should never be the stuff of teacher lounge gossip. Treat the private issues of your students with the same respect you would want others to afford your private issues.

13. Institute a policy of *alternative learning assignments* for students you know have cheated on a test or assignment. Let the students know that mastery of the information is the overriding issue and that another opportunity to demonstrate that mastery will be provided.

Also consider using homework as a means of *on-going information* on the progress of your students rather than as a source for grades. When parents, siblings, and peers might very well be part of a collaborative effort to help a student complete an assignment, it will be difficult to discern whether or not "cheating" occurred.

Similarly, *alternative assessment strategies* that take the place of testing will lessen the likelihood that cheating will result.

14. *Model respect* for the property of others by giving receipts to students when you must confiscate toys or other items that are creating a disruption. Let students know that the items will be returned to them at the end of the day when they bring you the receipt.

15. Teach students to chew gum and pass notes responsibly by using the guidelines of appropriate time, place,

and manner. Engage students in a discussion of when and how note passing and gum chewing would not violate any of the compelling state interest parameters.

16. Understand that *you are the model* in your classroom for trust and tolerance. Your students watch you and take their cues from your actions. As situations occur ask yourself, "What needs to be learned here? How can I respond in a way that will benefit all of us?"

Part Two

Judicious Discipline
in the Classroom—
Lesson Plans and Activities
for Building Democratic
Classroom Communities

Lessons, Units, and Activities
Presented in Five Categories:
Primary Classrooms
K through 8 Classrooms
Middle Level Classrooms
Secondary Classrooms
K through 12 Classrooms

Part Two

Judicious Discipline
in the Classroom

Primary Classrooms

(Activities Can Be Adapted for Higher Grades)

Building Respectful Communities in Primary Classrooms

Roberta Martel

A new school year begins. Preparations have been completed. Lesson plans are written, furniture and learning centers are in place, bulletin boards are thematically decorated, and students names are alphabetized on the word wall.

Seasoned teachers as well as new teachers realize that the most wonderfully written lesson plans and the most beautifully decorated classroom will not automatically assure a successful classroom environment where learning will take place for all students. Where in textbooks does it teach you what to do when Brandon, a second year kindergarten student, enters on the first day of school with a vacant look and a violent dislike for all the other students and any of your well-planned activities? How does a teacher engage students in a lesson when Chelsea, a new kindergarten student, is ceaselessly screaming, "I want my mommy"? This is exactly where the new challenge begins. The challenge of creating a safe, caring classroom environment where clear limits and boundaries are evident. Environments where students feel empowered to make "good choices" and are in control of their destinies.

As an elementary teacher for nearly 30 years, I set the tone for our learning environment in the very first minutes of that very first day of school. Through modeling of voice, facial gestures and words, children learn what the word respect looks like and sounds like. We cannot demand respect, we must create an atmosphere where students become a "family" celebrating individual differences and working together as a community. Respectful learning communities do not just happen; rather they are built carefully step-by-step.

The first step in creating this community of learners is to enlist the students to take part in writing the classroom rules followed by a discussion of fair consequences. Children thrive on routine and structure; therefore consistency with discipline delivered in a caring, respectful manner is critical. Knowing that everyone makes mistakes, I believe children deserve an opportunity to collect themselves and make good decisions about their actions. However, if the behavior continues, a visitor to my kindergarten classroom will hear the following statement, "Michael, you are not making a lovely choice."

If students need a further opportunity to reflect on behaviors and time to consider what are the best choices, I offer them a chance to sit by themselves while they read and reflect upon one of many poems I have posted around my room. The poems all have to do with treating others in respectful ways. In this case, a visitor to my room during group learning time might hear "Susan, I would like to invite you to a blue chair (all of the chairs in my classroom are blue, therefore the child chooses her own thinking spot), when you are ready to return as a great listener you may come back to join the rest of the family on the rug."

Children are very capable of behaving as responsible members of a classroom society as evidenced by observing students regrouping away from the rest of the class and then returning on their own to join in the activity. Through modeling I also set a tone of how my classroom should sound. Statements such as: " I like the way you are coloring" or " You make my heart happy" or " I can help you." I make it a point to use what I call "lovely words" throughout the day.

Educators have to work harder to establish their individual authority because the cultural foundations, belief systems, and family structures from which children come are so diverse. Many children come from homes where there is very little discipline or very violent forms of disciplining. Therefore, knowing your students is imperative to be able to individualize techniques while creating a working classroom environment. Children as well as adults do not respond well to being "backed against a wall." Brandon is a perfect example of a child who would not respond well to demands without choice. He would meet the demands by intensifying his angry behaviors. Coming from a very dysfunctional home environment, the coping tools that he brought to school were biting, punching, pinching, yelling, and ultimately running away. As his teacher, if I were to use intimidation and threats he would have responded with increased hostility. Instead, I chose to use a firm, yet low voice, reminding him to make good choices and, if necessary, an invitation to a blue chair. If he fought with me over leaving the group, I repeated the words, "You have made a sad choice. You may return as a learner when you are ready."

Establishing the home-school connection is imperative for a positive school experience for parents as well as their children. Being part of the team, parents can gain insight as to the techniques or tools used in the classroom and support the consistent message that is being established in school, "You are special and a wonderful member of our school 'family.'"

A good portion of my presentation on Back to School Night, the informational meeting for parents at the beginning of the new school year, is centered on modeling and discussing the techniques I use for classroom management. During my presentation, words, gestures, and methods are shared with parents and I encourage them to consider using the same words, gestures, or methods at home. I believe when we "speak the same language" and are consistent with our message, children will better understand their limits and boundaries. This presentation is followed up with one-on-one parent/teacher conferences where the individual needs of each child can be specifically addressed.

We as educators must assure parents, in a non-threatening way, that as a team we can help their child to feel success both academically and socially. When parents feel validated as the child's " first teacher" (whether a positive role model or not), windows of opportunity open for positive communication and ongoing dialogue. This dialogue is based on respect and an understanding of the diversity the parent and child bring to our classroom. Using active listening and non-judgmental strategies, a successful relationship can be built and nurtured with parents and children.

The old statement, "treat others as you would like to be treated," seems to be the foundation of my classroom discipline plan. Empowering students to be personally responsible and to help them work hard at being respectful members of the classroom/school community is the key for success!

Establishing *Judicious Discipline* in the Primary Classroom

From Ideas Originally Contributed by Margaret Abbott

Teaching Rights and Responsibilities

Age Group
K-3.

Objective
To assist students in the discovery of why rules are important. To help students understand that there are reasons for the rules that will guide classroom decisions during the year.

Time
First of two 3-minute sessions.

Materials
Crayons, paper, scissors, glue, large piece of butcher paper (cut to fit a bulletin board). An illustration of a scale and an actual scale.

Procedure (Part One)
Begin by having the students make small paper models of themselves. Have each student place their paper model on the actual scale. Put a paper model you have drawn on one side of the scale and have all the students put their models on the other. Tell

the students that the models represent a group of students and the trick is to balance the scales to make them equal or fair. Record their guesses on a sheet of poster paper and thank them for sharing their good ideas.

Ask one student to move his/her model from the scale pan with all the other models in it to the side with none. Ask students to think of ways they could have the scales balance. Suggest to them that everyday they enter school they are in an imaginary scale with the teacher balancing their individual rights with the needs of all students. Explain that the rights of each student and the needs of all students are difficult to balance without rules.

Ask students if they know what it means to have rights? What are rights? Discuss with them the rights they have: to be themselves, to be heard, and to be treated fairly. Be aware that children will often suggest rights they believe come to them from the Constitution, but in fact do not. (An example of this would be the right to a free, public education.) With third-graders, more time should be spent developing this distinction.

With young students end the lesson at this point.

Procedure (Part Two)

Have students brainstorm ways they can be themselves, ways they can be heard and ways they can be treated fairly. You can do this in a large group, or small groups—each small group would have one of the topics to brainstorm. Ask each small group to draw a picture of some of the ideas they brainstormed. Post the pictures and the brainstorms up around the room.

Go on to discuss what responsibilities they have in the classroom. Use a few examples to illustrate the concept of the scale. For instance, ask students if they think it would disturb their classroom if someone walked to the pencil sharpener. Then ask if there would be a problem if someone ran. Tip the scales on the individual side for walking, and on the other side for running. Running would be a violation of health and safety in the classroom and an individual student does not have the right to threaten the safety of others. It is the responsibility of each individual to move carefully for the good of everyone.

After a few of these examples, leave the scale as an example for the students to consider.

Review the rights that students have in the class and have children select to represent one of those rights with a drawing. Clearly explain that each child in the classroom has rights and that the single paper model on one side of the scale represents them. Glue the pictures on one side of the butcher paper.

End of session.

Teaching the Compelling State Interests

Age Group
K-3.

Objective
To help students understand their responsibilities in the classroom. To encourage students to help create classroom rules based on the Compelling State Interests.

Time
Thirty minutes again. The activity should begin sitting in a circle on the classroom rug or circle area.

Materials
Same as before.

Procedure (Part One)
Review the posters about rights you have put up around the room. Remind the students that you began by talking about the scale and how to make it balance. Ask "If you have the right to be yourself, does that mean you can do anything you want? Could you stand up and dance around the classroom and yell when we are all trying to work?" "Students will say "No!"

"What about being heard? Can you yell out anytime you want? What if we were in the library or working hard on our math lesson? What about being treated fairly? What would that look like? You all have rights but with rights come responsibilities or the need treat others the way we want to be treated. The way to remember our responsibilities is to have some rules in our classroom.

(Depending on the age of the students, you might want to stop here and do part two later.)

Procedure (Part Two)

"What kind of rules do we need?" "What rules would help our classroom to run smoothly and be a comfortable place for you?" "Do we need rules to help us stay safe?" "Should we have rules that protect our property, our stuff?" "Would it help us to learn better if we had a rule about why we are in school?" "Do we need a rule to keep students from disrupting our study and work time?"

The rules are based on the Compelling State Interests of Health and Safety, Property Loss and Damage, Legitimate Educational Purpose, and Serious Disruption (See *Judicious Discipline* [6th Ed.] by Forrest Gathercoal). With younger children, it would be appropriate to develop one concept at a time. For instance, health and safety could be the topic for one discussion session, saving the other Compelling State Interests for subsequent days.

Present the ideas of the Compelling State Interests. For instance, you might say "We all need to be safe. What rule could help us remember to keep ourselves and others safe?" A rule that says "Be safe" would be enough because you can have good discussions during class meetings on all the ways you can help yourselves and others to be safe.

Go on to discuss the other interests by asking students how they can all remember to respect the property of others as well as their own property. How can they help themselves and others to do their best work in school? How can they help themselves and others to keep their learning environment quiet and appropriate.

Procedure (Part Three)

After you have presented all the ideas behind all of the four Compelling State Interests, give the students a sheet of drawing paper and have them fold it in half. Ask them to draw two pictures. The first should be of someone breaking one of the rules they just developed and the second should be of someone respecting a rule. Before they begin drawing, brainstorm together some ideas for what a picture might look like that illustrated someone not being safe, or quiet, or respecting the property of others. Then discuss what a picture might look like of someone being careful, etc. Post the pictures around the rooms if students give you permission to do so.

Procedure (Part Four)

Bring out the scale again. This time explain that all students need to be safe and have their property protected and to be able to learn and to not be disrupted. But each one of them also has rights and those rights will always be respected. To dramatically demonstrate this concept, attach weights to the back of each of the figures you place on one side of the scale and a weight equal to all of the weights on the other side. For instance, place one figure representing each of the four rules with a one ounce weight attached to the back and place a figure on the other side of the scale with a four ounce weight attached. The point is that you want the scales to balance. Tell students that one important teacher responsibility is to try to keep the scales balanced at all times. Tell students that you will be discussing rights, responsibilities and how to keep the scales in balance during class meetings.

On the sheet of butcher paper mentioned earlier, write the word "Rights" over the first set of pictures. Display pictures of what should not be done in a classroom and title that section "Reason for Rules." Finally, put "Needs" over the pictures of how they would like the classroom to be.

Have students explain their drawings to you before posting them. (It is most important that you ask their permission 'before displaying any of their drawings. Ask for permission on a one-to-one basis.)

End of session.

Growing Ideas

Tammy Tasker

Big Idea

A community is shaped by all the individuals in a classroom. It grows out of relationships between teacher and individual children, and relationships among all the children. Trust is a critical ingredient in forming community. Talk and listening (dialogue) are necessary acts. Trust is valuing the learner as a human being, as one who has much to give, much to demonstrate, much to teach others (Avery, 1993). Creating a shared set of classroom values that promote respect for others' ideas is an essential aspect of participation as a class norm (Palincsar, Herrenkohl, 2002).

Objective

To demonstrate what happens when an idea is met with criticism, and when it is met with curiosity and encouragement. To stimulate a discussion of our responsibilities to each other as participants in a classroom community.

Materials

Small play people figures hidden inside a paper bag. Speech bubbles of written phrases such as "I noticed....," "I wonder....," "I thought....," "I liked....," "I learned....," "I discovered....," "I felt....," "I considered....," "Tell me more...," "I'm not sure what you mean...,"and "That's stupid," "That's dumb." Magazine photos or pictures from another source that can be easily folded many times over and have intrinsic appeal or inviting connotations for the students. Large and simple outline/map of the classroom drawn on butcher paper to serve as a story-telling mat.

Anticipatory Set/State Objective

"Today during our circle time, I will tell a story, and you will be able to watch the tiny characters as if you were watching a play. It may make you laugh and it may look very different from the stories we have been reading from books. But try to remember our ways of being polite listeners. After I tell this story, we will talk about what you noticed, what you are thinking. You will have a chance to try this way of telling stories yourself later today with the things I have brought."

Story

Act out a simple story using the toy figures of people. The story is set in the classroom during the opening meeting for the day. Represent children gathered for a classroom sharing circle. For instance, a story might begin: "Joe had a very small idea. He was just beginning to think it." (Lay the folded up picture on the rug next to Joe, to symbolize his newly-forming idea.) "He wanted to tell the people in his class about his idea, and he wanted to ask them some questions. He wanted to get some help with his idea. And this is what happened." Continue the narration of the story, following what happens as Joe tries to communicate his still-forming thoughts.

As the play figures in the circle make responses to Joe such as "I wonder...." or "I think....." the picture begins to unfold. But when Joe hears "that's stupid," the picture folds back up. Students will probably begin guessing what kinds of comments can cause the picture to unfold and what makes it fold back up again. Encourage their predictions.

In the end, have the positive, inquiring phrases outnumber the negative, so that Joe's idea unfolds for all to see. Encourage and facilitate a group discussion of the ways teachers and students can help ideas grow in the classroom. Make a wall chart of the "tell me more" responses that encourage participation and sharing of ideas in the classroom. Model additional ways to support the hard work of clarifying newly forming thoughts. Explore the idea that ideas can grow in complexity and richness within a supportive and respectful classroom community.

Reflection Questions/Closure
"Here is a map of our classroom. You can come to this map later and act out your own story with Joe and his friends. Could you tell a story here with one of your friends? If you come up with more ways to help ideas grow in our classroom while you are acting out your story, please work together to add them to our wall chart. You could also write about and draw your ideas in your journals."

Adaptations
This lesson relies on the children's abilities to understand story and analogy. Follow-up discussion and writing will allow the teacher to quickly evaluate students' understanding. More direct dialogue about how the folded up magazine picture represents an idea that is still forming in Joe's head could be needed.

References

Avery, C. (1993). *....And with a light touch: Learning about reading, writing, and teaching with first graders.* Portsmouth, NH: Heinemann.

Fisher, B. (1995). *Thinking and learning together: Curriculum and community in a primary classroom.* Portsmouth, NH: Heinemann.

Palincsar, A., & Herrenkohl, L. (2002). Designing collaborative learning contexts. *Theory into Practice, 41*(1).

Appreciating Diversity by Exploring Similarities and Differences

A. Ku'ulei Serna

Grade
  K-3.

Objectives
  1. To engage students in a mentally and emotionally healthy activity to practice behaviors indicating high self-esteem by developing a sense of uniqueness.
  2. To teach students to accept that people have different body shapes and sizes, and other personal characteristics that make them unique. (NHES 1/HECAT [MEH], grades K-4).
  3. To develop a students' senses of uniqueness by having students acknowledge the characteristics that make them unique. (NHES 1/HECAT [MEH], grades K-4).

Materials
  Children's book entitled *It's Okay To Be Different* by Todd Parr. Art supplies to create student portraits (paper, markers, paints, various materials, etc.).

Procedure
  Begin this lesson with a discussion. Ask students if they know anyone who looks or acts differently from them. Ask students to expound on their responses. Possible example questions: "Do you know of anyone who looks, acts or does things differently than

you?" "How are they different?" "What makes others different?" "How does that make you feel?"

After the opening discussion, introduce the children's book *It's Okay To Be Different* by Todd Parr. You may want to give students an overview of the book and what you expect them to pay close attention to while you read (optional).

Read the book and facilitate discussions that emphasize the positive notion that "It's okay to be different." Have students discuss personal and relevant experiences relating to the differences emphasized in the book. Stress the importance of accepting differences of others. Have students begin thinking about what makes them unique and different from others (e.g., physical traits, interests, talents, hobbies, likes and dislikes, etc.). You may want to have students randomly share beginning ideas about personal differences or may want students to share at the end of the lesson.

After reading the book and holding a brief discussion, have students create portraits of themselves. Begin by having students pair up. Have one member of each pair lie down on a piece of butcher paper while his or her partner traces the body. Have them switch and repeat the process. Then each student will have a life size portrait to color, paint, and decorate. Emphasize that the portraits they are creating should make clear what they feel is unique about them. Have the students title their portrait, "It's Okay for (Student Name) To Be Different."

Have the students share their portrait in a classroom community circle and then display them around the room. If this is done early in the year, it will also help the class to learn each other's names. On a separate sheet of paper have them complete the statement, "I am different because...........and it's okay to be different." They can dictate the sentence or use inventive spelling.

Closure

When all students have shared their portrait, call a class meeting. During the meeting, ask them to point out the differences amongst themselves as a class. Remember to emphasize that they are to accept the differences of others. Also, reiterate the importance of being unique, and that students should enjoy being different.

Lesson Plan
for Inclusive Environment
(Integration of Language Arts, Science, Math,
Social Studies, Health, and Art)

Younghee Kim

Topic
Fruit Seed Investigation.

Theme
Diversity.

Age Group
Pre K-3.

Objective
To learn about the diversity of many aspects of our lives. Individuals need to appreciate and work together with everyone's differences and talents and gifts. Differences in us are natural and need to be appreciated.

Time
30-45 minutes.

Materials
Seeds of different fruits—Apple, pear, orange, grapes, peach, watermelon, honey dew melon, cantaloupe, strawberry, tomato, avocado, papaya, guava (whatever fruits are available depending on the season and region).
Paper plates and safe knives (for adult use).

133

Anticipatory Set

Bring out different types of fruits and talk about color, taste, smell, texture, shape, season, characteristics or fruit personalities. Discuss how these differences bring all kinds of tastes and nutrition needs of our body.

Procedure

1. Take each fruit and cut each in half so that the inside seeds will show.
2. Take out only the seeds parts and display in small paper dishes.
3. Look, touch, smell, taste, cut more if desired.
4. Introduce the color and artistic nature of fruits and have them draw and describe the tastes of their favorite fruit.
5. If desired, teacher may facilitate the students to make fruit salad and talk about all the steps of making: wash, peel, cut, and prepare for school snack.

Closure

Review with the students or ask questions around the following key concepts as developmentally appropriate:

How do we appreciate diversity of fruits or foods in our life?

How can we best appreciate and share the different tastes of fruits available to individuals?

How do these fruits help us to appreciative of the cycles of season, weather, water, growers, and earth?

How do different individuals compose our society and make it harmonized?

How can each of us best support, enjoy, and celebrate the diverse nature of life?

Adaptation for Students with Special Needs

The teacher may need to assist some students with disabilities as needed (e.g., cutting, peeling, investigation of seeds, washing the fruits for snack preparation).

Variations

Expand to other diverse materials or subjects—vocations, clothing, inventions, foods, weather, learning styles, hobbies, sports, visual arts, performing arts, musical instruments, people, animals, houses, and more.

Judicious Discipline
in the Classroom

K-8 Classrooms

(Activities Can Be Adapted for Higher Grades)

Defining Rights
and Democratic Values

From a Unit Originally Contributed
by Anne Marie Strangio

Introduction

In my work with high-risk 4th and 5th graders, I needed a format for both presenting *Judicious Discipline* as my classroom management ideal, and for empowering my students by teaching them about their rights and responsibilities and asking them to take charge of their own lives.

The following set of lesson plans is designed for teachers at the intermediate level to introduce *Judicious Discipline* at the beginning of the school year. It covers the main ideas, giving students a broad based understanding to begin the year. The unit is only an introduction. In order to fully and effectively implement *Judicious Discipline*, the unit should be followed by regularly scheduled class meetings.

It is most important that a teacher committed to the ideals of *Judicious Discipline* hangs on to her/his beliefs through any testing students might do and continues teaching in a way that is democratic and student-centered. When students realize that the teacher is truly their advocate and not trying to "trick" them, they will approach the classroom with greater confidence and have a great deal of "buy-in" and interest in what's being taught.

Lesson #1
Defining Rights and Democratic Values

Objective

This lesson is a brainstorm, class discussion, and small group discussion about defining what rights are and what the democratic values of our country and community are.

Rationale

Before students begin learning what rights citizens have, and the history of those rights, they all need a common base for understanding the concepts of rights and the democracy that ensures those rights.

Materials

Poster paper, tape, and markers, and white board.

Logistics

This lesson takes one to two class periods of 1-1/2 hours each. Students should be sitting in small groups to facilitate whole-class discussions and small group discussions.

Group Process

Assign group roles, such as recorder, group leader and other roles necessary to completing the task. Review expectations for group communication and what people in the various roles will be responsible for.

Overview Mental Set

Pass out the Civil Rights and Democratic Values handout. Explain to students that this is an outline of things that we absolutely need to cover, but that they will be directing the lessons by their questions and issues that they want to learn about. For instance, you might say, "I only have these four items which we must learn about, so you (students) should ask all the clarifying questions you might have and raise other issues that occur to you." Let students know that you might not be able to discuss all the issues or answer all the questions, but what does not get addressed in this lesson will be saved for class meeting topics.

Begin by telling students they should write some notes by each of the items on the handout as they learn about them. "To begin with, we're going to talk about the first item on the handout: The definition of rights and democratic values." This will be good research and note-taking practice.

Brainstorm Mental Set

"We are going to be studying all kinds of rights, where they came from, and what they mean. We will be beginning with a brainstorm about the rights we have."

Modeling/Guided Practice

Model a couple of rights for the students. Write on the white board: "Read whatever I want." Say out loud: "I have the right to read whatever I want. Any book, any newspaper, any magazine." Then ask out loud: "Why do I have this right?" Explain to students that if they think they know why during their own brainstorm, to write it down on their list. Ask students for another right and write it on the white board. When it looks like they understand, begin the small group brainstorm.

Small Group Student Activity

Small group brainstorm: Ask students to brainstorm at their table groups, all the rights they think they have and record their work on a sheet of poster paper. If they seem to be getting stuck, have them begin with rights they have in the classroom. Also have them start thinking about why they have the rights which they write down.

Activity Closure

Give students a two-minute notice to finish up their brainstorms. Then ask them to send one representative up to the front of the room and post their sheet of poster paper.

Class Discussion Mental Set

Say to the students "Let's look at all the rights we wrote down." Allow them to make comments and observations. Cross out any duplications students note. After they are finished, ask them to help make a class definition for what rights are.

Guided Practice

"So, what are rights?" Have the students work with you to categorize the rights under the headings of Freedom (The right to be yourself), Justice (The right to be heard or have a voice), and Equality (The right to be treated fairly.) If something the students wrote down does not fit under any of the headings, determine as a class if it really is a right? For instance, there is no "right" to an education, but it is compulsory in all 50 states.

Small Group Student Activity

Based on the class discussion, ask students to work in their small groups to develop q definition of rights. Have a couple of students look the word "rights" up in the dictionary, CD ROM, etc. and share their findings with their groups.

Activity Closure

Return to the whole group with definitions. "Let's review your suggestions and see if we can agree on a single definition." By the end of the discussion, the class should have a solid "working" definition of rights.

Lesson #2
Compelling State Interests

◆ Definition of Rights

◆ Compelling State Interests:
   Property Loss and Damage
   Legitimate Educational Purpose
   Health and Safety
   Serious Disruption

◆ Rights and Responsibilities:
Compulsory education
Who has the rights?
The balance
Time, place, and manner

Objective
Students will learn about the four compelling state interests which govern our society. They will demonstrate their learning by applying the language of the compelling state interests to rules developed for your classroom.

Rationale
It is important for students to understand where rules come from, and why they exist. Our society uses just four basic rules or interests to secure the common welfare. It is sensible to teach basic rules and use them as a foundation for classroom rules. These compelling state interests are the balance for rights that students have, and are a necessary for understanding rights and responsibilities.

Materials
White board, paper and pencil, copies of your school's rules for each student, a spelling and vocabulary list for each student, and the Compelling State Interests worksheet (at end of lesson).

Logistics
This lesson will take one to two class periods of 1-1/2 hours each. Students should be sitting in their table groups to facilitate whole-class discussions and small group discussions.

Enrichment Activity
Ask students to work in their small groups to complete the Compelling State Interests. Tell them when they have completed the worksheet they should share examples of seeing people doing things that violate the compelling state interests.

Class Discussion Mental Set

Write "Four Compelling State Interests" on the white board. Have students work in their small groups to define the term. Encourage them to look up words they are not sure about. Explain to students that these are basically the foundation for all rules in our society. "Our government has given us certain rights, like the ones we brainstormed earlier. The four compelling state interests are the laws which limit our rights so everyone can be safe and protected. We will use these same rules in our classroom so you will learn and experience everyday how our society works. This is your opportunity to learn citizenship and my opportunity to help you learn how to be an effective citizen.

Presentation

Write the compelling state interest on the white board: health and safety, property loss and damage, serious disruption, legitimate educational purpose. Have students work in their own groups to come up with examples they know about from the community and the school. For instance, an example of a rule for health and safety would be a stop sign.

Class Discussion

Share what was discussed in the groups. What examples did they come up with? Which compelling state interest did they have trouble identifying an example for? Make sure at the end of the discussion that they understand the meaning and at least one application for each of the interests.

Activity Closure

Reflect back to students and have them answer as a group: "So if I make a classroom rule saying 'move safely from one place to another, what compelling state interest am I referring to?" Give a few examples, and then definitions for them to respond to.

Worksheet
on Compelling State Interests and School Rules

Health and Safety

Property Loss and Damage

Seriousd Disruption

Legitimate Educational Purpose

Analyzing School Rules

Giving Directions

Ask students to refer to the worksheet on Compelling State Interests. Pass out a copy of the school rules, poster paper, and markers to each group. Tell students that they are going to be doing two activities which you are going to explain now so they can just move to the second when they are ready. The first activity is to read the school rules in their table groups and make sure that everyone understands them.

The second activity is to work in their groups to determine which school rules go under which heading on their worksheets.

Activity

In their groups, the reader will read the school rules, the leader will lead the discussion and the recorder will place the rules under the heading selected by the group.

Ask the groups to determine which state interest has the most rules? The least? Are there rules which fall into more than one category?

Activity Closure

Ask students to share what they found with their table group by posting their papers up around the room. See if there are any rules which students put in different categories. Give them about five minutes to discuss, then return to the whole group and share anything that surprised them, stood out, etc. At the end of the activity they should turn in their worksheets.

Students will probably be able to come up with good examples for property loss and damage, health and safety, and serious disruption, but may have a hard time coming up with rules for legitimate educational purpose.

If they have not found examples of rules that fit Legitimate Educational Purpose, you can talk about homework assignments, curriculum, linking lessons to standards—all of which will help them understand the importance of this compelling interest.

Lesson #3
Balance of Rights and Responsibilities
and Compulsory Education

Objective

Students will understand the balance of rights and responsibilities.

Rationale

It is important for students to understand why they have to be in school every day, and what the ramifications of that are. They also need to understand their end of the bargain when granted rights. This lesson will give them a deeper understanding of their rights, and their social responsibilities.

Materials

White board, original brainstorm list of rights prominently displayed, paper and pencil.

Logistics

This lesson will take a class period of 1-1/2 hours. Students should be sitting in their groups to facilitate whole-class discussions and small group discussions.

Introduction

"We are endowed with these rights, but they can be limited to protect everybody's need to be safe and undisrupted." If the group does not select a right you feel should be discussed, add it to the list by highlighting it. Lead students to the concept of balance between rights and responsibilities.

Group Activity and Discussion

Have one of the students pick three or four rights from their brainstormed list of rights. Highlight them ones selected. Then ask students to work in their groups and identify the responsibilities which balance the rights they selected. Students should be able to come up with many. Have them record their work on a sheet of paper to share with the class in a follow-up discussion.

Activity Closure

Have students come back together as a whole class and share some of the balances they discovered. Which rights had the most responsibilities? Are some more important than others? Are they all of equal importance?

Lesson #4
Time, Place, and Manner

Introduction

When we think about how our rights are always balanced with our responsibilities, there are three words that can help us remember the balance. They are time, place and manner.

Group Activity and Discussion

Ask students what they think Time would mean. Say "Can you run when you are at school? Do you have to walk all the time? What about when you are at recess? In what place is it important to use quiet voices? What place would be appropriate for loud voices? If you are upset with me or another person, what is the appropriate manner?

Small Group or Independent Student Activity

Ask students to continue this activity in their small groups. They should come up with an appropriate time, place, and manner for each of the rights they listed in the previous activity. Make sure each group has a leader, time keeper, recorder and mediator who addresses any disagreements about what should or should not be recorded.

Activity Closure

Have students come back together as a whole class and share some of the time, place, and manner issues that they brainstormed.

Lesson #5
Protected Classes

Protected Classes:
    Race
    National Origin
    Religion
    Sex
    Age
    Handicap
    Marital Status
    Sexual Orientation (In some states)
What does this look like? Where do you fit in?

Objective

Students will learn about the protected classes (categories) that protect us all from discrimination.

Rationale

It is important for students to learn about discrimination and how they and other people are protected from it. This could also tie in to studies of post-civil war United States History with regards to African-American history, Native-American history, women's rights, etc.

Materials

White board, art supplies (magazines, construction paper, glue, crayons, markers, scissors, etc.), paper and pencil. Construction paper should already have the heading "We Do Not Discriminate."

Logistics

This lesson should take two class periods of 1-1/2 hours each. Students should be sitting in their groups to facilitate whole-class discussions and small group discussions.

Mental Set

Write "Protected Classes" on the white board. Have students help to define the words, emphasizing the use of the word classes as meaning "type" and not "course of study."

Presentation

The law protects us from discrimination by defining each of us seven different ways. This is not about special groups—the protected classes describe all of us. Explain to students that no one in the United States, us included, can be discriminated against for the following things: Age, handicap, marital status, race, national origin, religion, and gender and, in some states, sexual orientation. Write them on the board one at a time and discuss what each is. Emphasize that we all have a race, a national origin and a marital status. We are all able or disabled and can be both. For instance, we might have an accident that makes us temporarily disabled but when we heal we are able again.

Ask students to get into their groups. Pass out the art supplies. Ask each group to find pictures of as many of the protected classes as they can. Have them cut out the pictures and mount them on the construction paper in a collage. Tell them the collage also has to include all seven (or eight—if your state recognizes sexual orientation) of the protected classes. Have the students post their collages around the room.

Lesson #6
Current Rights Issues

Objective

Students will find current rights issues from the newspaper and magazines. They will then identify what the issues are, who has what rights, and which direction they think the balance should tip. They will also learn about the "gray" area of rights issues, and discover that there are often no clear, easy answers. Ultimately, students will participate in a debate about one of the rights issues which touches them and they will learn about debate format and etiquette.

Rationale

It is important for students to be informed about current events, and they should be thinking about and reflecting upon how these events affect them and the world around them. It is also pertinent that students understand that the world, much like the classroom, operates in a "gray" area, sometimes without clear solutions. Learning debate skills is a great way for students to learn constructive arguing and critical and logical thinking.

Materials

Newspapers and magazines, copies of articles which we use, 3x5 note cards, white board.

Logistics

This lesson will be in two parts. In part one, the small groups will be identified as debate teams. Ideally, each group will be made up of four to five people. Each group will select an issue they find in the newspapers or magazines provided for them. Emphasize that one half of the team will argue the pro side of the issue and the other will argue against it. Make it clear that it does not matter how students personally feel about any issue. The point of debate is to demonstrate a depth of understanding regardless of personal feelings.

Activity

In small groups, have students scan the papers and magazines for articles that interest them. When they have selected three or four, ask them to show the articles to you and work with them to select their debate topic. This gives you an opportunity to monitor the issues and make sure they are selecting topics that are age appropriate.

When every group has selected a topic, review the expectations for computer research. Make sure all students understand the rules about which sites are appropriate for research and which are not. Ask them what they should do if they stumble on a site that has adult content. Remind students to take notes on their topics rather than printing out article. Provide them with note cards for this purpose.

Debate Proposals

Ask the groups to consider why their topic is a rights issue? What is the issue? What would be the pro side of the issue? What would be the opposition to the issue? Ask them to answer the questions and submit their debate proposals by the end of the time set aside for this activity. This will give you time to review their proposals and offer suggestions for further research, if necessary.

Debate (Day One)

Mental Set

Remind students that they are going to be debating not arguing. What is the difference? Show a brief clip from CSPAN of a congressional debate. Do not use a clip from a news show that uses confrontation as this would not be an appropriate model for what you want students to learn.

Preparation

Explain the debate procedure you're going to use and write it on the board at the same time. The pro team will always go first, the con team second. Both teams will have three minutes for opening arguments, five minutes for main arguments, three minutes for rebuttal, and two minutes for closing. Define what each of those things are, and give a mini-demonstration.

In their groups, have students develop scoring rubrics for the debate. Rubrics might include criteria such as: Kept within the allotted time; Points were made clearly; Courtesy was shown for the other opinion; The conclusion effectively wrapped up the main points; etc. Have all groups submit their suggestions for the rubric. Tell them you will be handing out the final copy tomorrow. Review and incorporate as many of their ideas into the rubric as possible.

Debate (Day Two)

Activity

Distribute copies of the rubric to all students. Ask them to review all the criteria and levels in their groups before moving on with their research and preparation. Circulate to see if there are any questions about what is expected.

Students will have the rest of the class period to prepare their arguments, then part of the next day to polish them. The debates will be presented after the students have had a chance to polish them. At this point, have the teams divide up so each side can practice away from the other side.

They need to decide who will speak, if they want one or two representatives, or if they want to dole out the speaking roles. Suggest to them as you are circulating that they should do a mini-preparation of what they think the other team is going to say so that they can be prepared to rebut it.

Process

Students will work in their groups preparing their arguments. Spend time circulating and helping them with individual problems, as well as making sure that all students are participating.

The Debate

The students who are participating in the first debate will sit in a row on opposite sides. The rest of the students will be their audience, and two students will be the timekeepers. Review the rules which were set up earlier (such as no interrupting, no personal attacks, etc.).

Closure

Gather students back into a whole class. What did they think? Was it effective? How did they feel when the other team rebutted them? Answer questions and let students speak.

The "Rights" Song

Rights, rights, we all have rights.
Short people, tall people,
Dark people, light people,
Big people, small people,
Black people, white people.
It's neat that all people
Become the right people
Because they all have rights.
Right!

Rights
Spelling and Vocabulary List

Educators can post this list for students to use when writing reflections about the unit on rights. Some of the words might be used as spelling lists or bonus words for spelling lists.

amendments
assembly
authority
civil rights
compulsory
confidentiality
consequences
constitution
democracy
democratic
disability
discrimination
disruption
educational
equality
equity
ethical
ethics
freedom
illegal
immunity
individual
judicious
justice
legitimate
liberty
marital status
national origin
privacy
probable cause
procedural due process

protected classes
protection
reasonable
religion
responsibilities
responsibility
Supreme Court
tolerance

Enrichment Activity

In my classroom we play a fun "filler" game when we have a few minutes to kill called "Don't Break The Rule." I present the students with an arbitrary rule and they try and think of all they ways they can get around it. At the end of the game we identify what the real issue or compelling state interest is that might cover that rule. They love this game! Not only are they using rule-breaking skills which they have mastered despite our best efforts, it very clearly shows them what the real issues are behind the seemingly arbitrary rules they encounter daily.

For example, I may write the following on the board: "No gum chewing in class."

Their responses have been: "I'm not chewing it; I'm just sucking on it." "You're not actually teaching right now, so it's not class time." "It's not really gum." "You didn't say anything about not gum eating; I'm planning on swallowing this piece." "I have a medical condition with my ears popping, so I have to." "I'm just holding it or I'm just playing with it."

When I try and narrow it down for a bit more of a challenge, they get even more outrageous, but wholly committed to their right-ness: "No gum in class."

They respond: "This is just flavored rubber, not gum." (Swallow) "Gum? I don't have any gum." "I can't sit at this desk because there's gum stuck underneath it and I don't want to get accused of having gum in class!"

The students give an excellent illustration of how many of them operate when they come across rules they perceive to be contrived and unfair. At the end of the game we would try and decide what the rule's author's real intent was with that rule. For the no-gum rule, one of my classes decided that the real issues were property loss and damage—because of kids leaving gum under desks and chairs and in the carpet; health and safety—if kids were being active while chewing gum they could choke; and serious disruption—if kids were popping bubbles or taking their gum out of their mouth to play with it.

This is good stuff! Once they realized and verbalized what the real issues were, they were then willing to work within the intended parameters of the rule. And when I did see a student inappropriately chewing gum, I could simply ask them what the real issue was and respond as a guide and not as an autocratic finger-pointer.

The real issue for us as educators is empowerment, and by empowering children we are requiring them to be in charge of their own behavior and learning, and are helping them to be participating citizens in our classrooms and in their lives. These skills they learn within the school walls will serve them well when they leave the building and become participating citizens of our world.

Establishing Commensurate and Compatible Consequences

Margaret Abbott

Age Group
 4th-6th grade.

Objective
 To establish a set of consequences for inappropriate behaviors.

Time
 20 to 25 minutes.

Procedure
 Teacher says "We have discussed how we expect people to behave and we have created a set of rules to remind us of that discussion. But sometimes people will forget. When that happens, I will work with those people to help them remember our rules and help them understand why it is important to follow the rules. On occasion, it may be necessary for the people who broke a rule to experience a consequence that will help them do better next time.

 "Because I want to help you remember the rules and learn how to follow them, I will work with you to make sure that the consequence fits whatever rules have been broken. Consequences in this classroom will be commensurate—that means they will have something to do with the rule that has been broken. For instance, if one of you decided to dump out the wastebasket on to the floor, what do you think would be a commensurate consequence?"

Listen to responses, giving them feedback on their comments. Then say "There will be a second part to consequences in this classroom. I want to help you remember the rules, but I also always want you to feel good about who you are and to know that I want you to succeed. Because that is important to me, I will make sure that the consequences you experience will not embarrass you. In your small groups, please spend the next five minutes brainstorming what would and what would not be embarrassing. It is important for me to hear how you feel about this, so together we can make decisions you will be comfortable with if there is a problem. "If the time comes that a consequence is necessary, I will talk privately with the student who has broken a rule. Together we will discuss the commensurate and compatible parts of the consequence."

Let students brainstorm in their groups for the next five minutes. Get the class back together. Put two categories on the board—"Embarrassing" and "Not Embarrassing." Have the students' list their ideas under the proper categories. When every group has posted its list, talk about what the lists have in common. Take the common elements from the list and create a poster that has as its heading, "I will never...." Then list the things students would see as embarrassing. For instance the poster might say "I will never...put your name on the board. I will never....make fun of you."

You might want to include language from the "I will never..." poster in your statement of ethics. The "I will never...." poster should also be the guideline for the students' statement of ethics. After all, if they do not want to be embarrassed by you, they should not embarrass or tease or tattle on each other.

Equity in Mathematics and Science

Incorporating Materials Originally Contributed by Karen Higgins

> *Judicious Discipline* requires a genuine commitment and conscientious effort to assure all students an equal opportunity for success. (Forrest Gathercoal, 1990, p. 102)

In today's classrooms, mathematics and science—as well as language arts—have become the focus, some might say, battleground of No Child Left Behind. The ability of all students to quickly master concepts and factoids in mathematics and science and then demonstrate their learning in high stakes testing situations has shaken the spirit of equal educational opportunity to its core. The struggle to ensure equity in mathematics and science is not only related to gender but also to socio-economics and first language issues.

Dr. Karen Higgins provided *Practicing Judicious Discipline* with some activities to promote equal access to these who content areas. While the activities originally targeted gender equity but, as is true with all good teaching tools, they will help students across the spectrum of needs, abilities, and diversity.

Equity Issues

Each one of the three activities below addresses an equity issue.[1] These issues are highlighted here and should help you do the following for your students: (a) heighten the awareness of the issues, and (b) provide a rationale as to the value and purpose of the activity. Lesson plans for each issue appear on the pages that follow.

Activity #1:
Social Pressures and Behavior

Issue: *Social Pressures*

Success and achievement in mathematics are usually considered to be associated more with males in than females, more with Caucasian students than students of Color and more with those students coming from homes of economic privilege. Female students acquire the notion that they will be perceived as brainy or nerds if they succeed in mathematics or outperform boys. Popular media underscores these misperceptions. These stereotypes have the potential to create conflicts for girls who enjoy mathematics. The conflicts are further complicated for women from cultures where mathematics is discouraged because it is viewed as unnecessary or even unfeminine for women. Teachers must involve all students in learning that mathematics and science are areas where success is expected and respected.

Activity #2:
Draw a Scientist

Issue: *Understanding Stereotypes in the Media*

Media— movies, television, radio, newspapers, magazines, books, computer software, and others—have a strong influence on our students and have the ability to affect perceptions of appropriate careers. When students see the vast majority of scientists as White and male, they view this as descriptive of reality. Choosing a career is one of life's most important decisions and too often it is made quickly with little information. The annual earnings of careers related to mathematics and science are the highest of all professional level occupations. Teachers can help students better understand their own misperceptions by recognizing the stereotypes and then working to alter their understandings of who is and can be a scientist.

Activity #3:
Creating a Bulletin Board

Issue: *Invisibility of Contemporary Role Models*

Students of Color, female students, and students from low socio-economic backgrounds often believe that mathematics and science are areas of study not open to general participation. Unfortunately, the media images of contemporary mathematicians and scientists reinforce this belief. If teachers want all students to perceive themselves as potential mathematicians and scientists, then they need to expose them to suitable role models.

Note

[1] The starter ideas for many of these activities came from the "Teacher Education Equity Project"; Center for Advanced Study in Education; City University New York Graduate Center.

References

Gathercoal, F. (2004). *Judicious discipline* (6th Ed.). San Francisco: Caddo Gap Press.

Grossman, H., & Grossman, S. H. (1994). *Gender issues in education.* Needham Heights, MA: Allyn & Bacon.

Wellesley College Center for Research on Women. (1992). *How schools shortchange girls.* Washington, DC: American Association of University Women Educational Foundation.

Activity #1:
Social Pressures and Behavior

Age Group
5th to 12th grade.

Objective
To expose students to stereotypical attitudes they might hold towards people who are successful with mathematics.

Time
One hour.

Materials
Popular magazines, glue, poster board for collages.

Procedure
1. Ask students to write a list of adjectives they think describes a typical student in their grade level. Brainstorm some adjectives with them to get this activity started.
2. Have students read their lists and generate a class list of characteristics. Ask the students if the characteristics can be clustered under a heading such as Gender Traits. Ask the students to see how many headings they can come up with and which descriptors go under which heading.
3. Post their work around the room and have students look at the work that has been posted. What sort of stereotypes emerge from the terms and the ways in which the terms have been clustered? Compare the traits and discuss how the descriptions reflect social pressures and how they affect mathematics learning in the classroom.
4. Have students look through magazines which are popular for their grade levels. They should find and cut out pictures which illustrate and reinforce these stereotypical characteristics. They should also look for pictures that do not characterize these stereotypical traits.
5. In small groups, students should assemble collages that illustrate these stereotypical and/or non-stereotypical traits. Students should discuss how these images influence behaviors and expectations, even in very subtle ways.

6. Students could also search newspapers and popular magazines for articles and photographs of people working in mathematics and related fields. Ask students to count the following: The number of women and men pictured in illustrations; The number of People of Color pictured in the illustrations; The number of women and men listed as authors of articles.

7. In small groups, have students present their findings to the class. Have them develop some form of graph to show what they discovered

Activity #2:
Draw a Scientist

Age Group
K to 12th grade.

Objective
To confront students' perceptions of scientists and stimulate thoughts regarding the stereotypes students often hold which are related to careers in these fields.

Time
Approximately one hour.

Materials
Blank drawing paper, pencils or other drawing utensils, tape, crayons, or colored pencils. Optional: graph paper.

Procedure
1. Pass out the materials listed above to each student or have a supply of materials for table groups.

2. Ask students to draw their common perceptions of a scientist without discussing the project first with fellow classmates. (If you are working with students who do not feel comfortable drawing pictures, ask them to write a physical description of their scientist.)

3. Have students give their scientist a name and age and write a description of what he/she does for a living.

4. When drawings and descriptions are complete, tape them to the wall or on a bulletin board so all can see.

5. Ask questions, such as the following, to increase students' awareness of stereotypes: How many drew males? females? What races are represented (or what cultural generalizations can be made) by the people in the pictures? (Are they mostly White males?) How many are wearing white lab coats? How many have wild hair, like Einstein? How many have glasses? How many look like "nerds?" How many have a blackboard in their picture with incomprehensible formulas written on it? How many figures have pocket protectors? What ages are represented?

6. Have students to tally frequencies related to the above responses and graph the results. This could also be done in small groups with each group choosing a particular category and doing a more thorough analysis of the pictures. Display the graphs in your classroom.

7. Engage the class in a discussion about their pictures and perceptions. You may want to ask questions such as the following: Why conclusions can they draw? What influences their perceptions of scientists? Is it possible for these perceptions to influence career choices? Why/why not? (After all, who wants to be a nerd wearing a lab coat with a pocket protector?)

This is an excellent assessment activity for teachers who wish to gain insights into their students' perceptions of and dispositions towards careers related to science.

Activity #3
Creating a Bulletin Board

Age Group
2nd to 10th grade.

Objective
To expose students to contemporary mathematicians and scientists as a way of encouraging all students to continue their studies in mathematics and science.

Time
Approximately one hour.

Concept

Many teachers like to have their classrooms decorated when students walk into class the first day. Other teachers enjoy giving students ownership in creating the classroom environment. This activity would make a great beginning of the year activity that sets the stage for creating an equitable learning environment with your students.

Materials

Newspapers and magazines; scissors.

Procedure

1. Arrange your students in pairs. As much as possible, try to pair up students so that each pair will be as diverse as possible. Pass out the newspapers and magazines to your students.

2. Have students search these publications for articles and photographs of any mathematicians, scientistss and related fields they find.

3. As students become engaged in the activity, walk around the room and listen to their conversations. Make sure they are cutting out all the applicable pictures not just those of stereotypical images.

Jotting down their comments and sharing them during the discussion could add another dimension to the activity as well as provide valuable insights for you as a teacher.

4. Have your students create a bulletin board in the classroom using the pictures and other art supplies.

Make sure that women of Color are clearly represented in the bulletin board display.

5. Discuss with the students what they found in the magazines/newspapers and why they think you chose to engage them in the activity. There is research to support that leveling with students is a very successful strategy since equity should not be a secret goal but one shared with students (Sadker, M., & Sadker, D., 1994).

6. Ask students to reflect on the activity in their journals. Reading their reflections will help you become more aware of your students' beliefs about their perceptions of what it means to have equal opportunity.

Follow-Up Activity

1. Invite a mathematician and a scientist to class. Make sure that these guests are People of Color and/or women. In other words, these guests should counter rather than reinforce stereotypes.

2. Have students generate a list of interview questions prior to the visit. Students may want to ask the guests to talk about their career paths and prospects, and describe what it is like for them to be in their fields.

3. Interview the guests.

4. Have students discuss and reflect on what they learned, orally and in writing.

Reference

Sadker, M., & Sadker, D. 1994. *Failing at fairness: How our schools cheat girls.* New York: Touchstone.

Community Citizenship

*Ideas for This Community Activity Have Been Developed
from Materials Originally Submitted by Betty Powers*

Creating climates for classroom equity means appreciating,
understanding and respecting differences. One way teachers can
do that is by developing activities that are inclusive rather than
exclusive, particularly around holiday seasons. What follows is
one suggestion for ways that students can work together to serve
their communities and maintain the wholesome neutrality of a
democratic classroom.

Judicious Discipline can and should extend from the classroom out into the community. Learning tolerance and how to
make responsible decisions becomes very relevant when students are faced with real situations.

Age Group
4th through 6th graders. (This would be very appropriate for
other grades as well.)

Goal
To broaden the students' concepts of responsible classroom
citizenship to include participatory community citizenship.

Objectives
Students will:
1. Acquire an understanding of, and interest in, their local
community.

2. Develop and organize community service projects.
3. Cultivate a feeling of commitment to their community.
4. Heighten their sense of civic ethics.
5. Generate active and responsible civic behavior and involvement in local issues.

Procedure

The activities should address community needs. Curriculum can be integrated by having students research and develop needs they have discovered in their community. Then the class or several classes might work together to sponsor school-wide activities as they become aware of local needs. These might include winter clothing drives, canned food drives, packing pencil boxes for other students, writing to people in nursing homes, and staging school-wide clean ups.

Have students sign up for the project they would most like to work on each term. Working on the projects can be a sponge activity. In other words, when students have finished an assignment before others are done, they can work on one of the projects. The projects could also be worked on as one of the learning centers in a classroom.

Projects

The research students did in preparation will identify the community needs and the projects for addressing those needs. Below are some suggestions but these are only suggestions. Remember that these activities serve the purpose of building and sustaining equity because they will be done instead of holiday-based activities.

Winter Clothing Drive

This type of project is especially necessary where winters are very cold. Items of clothing can be distributed to a number of different organizations that help people in need.

Activity Boards

These toys are made from patterns for a quiet book. Students attach flannel pieces, "googly" eyes, and ribbons to tag board. The toys help small children learn to tie, button, and braid.

Books

Students create their own stories as part of a small-group activity. The stories are written, illustrated, and bound with spiral backs. Students donate their books to different organizations working with children. These organizations should be community-based rather than faith-based. Homeless shelters and safe houses would be worthy recipients. Also children's wards in hospitals would be very happy to have such donations.

Decorations

Students use their creative talents to brighten up shelters, clinics, and senior residences.

How Is Art a Part of My Life?
A Unit for K to 8 Students

Jennifer Herring

Overview

This unit is designed to establish a foundation in the visual arts for teachers and their students who want to work together in a democratic classroom environment that values different ways of knowing, provides empowering experiences in the visual arts, exhibits student work and engages students in personal reflection. This unit includes six major projects in the visual arts that build on the main question, "How is Art a Part of My Life?" and uses the following questions to guide our study:

1. Who Am I as An Artist and How are the Arts a Part of My Life?
2. What's the Big Idea?
3. Who's Art Is It?
4. What Do I Want to Create?
5. Where Can I Share My Artwork with Others?
6. Will You Come to Our Art Opening?

These experiences are a great way to get to know more about ourselves and each other, to understand how the visual arts are a part of our lives, to learn more about other artists, to develop the skills needed to use the visual arts as a form of communication, to reflect on our artwork, and to share our work with others.

These projects are designed to build on each other to provide teachers and students powerful experiences in the visual arts that are connected to their own lives and their own understanding. Each experience can be modified to meet the needs for specific grades levels. These experiences are written for eighth grade students and a kindergarten modification id shared for each project to demonstrate how the these concepts are adapted for younger students and developed to accommodate the needs of each student in your inclusive classroom.

The first project—"Who Am I as An Artist and How are the Arts a Part of My Life?"—is the foundation for the research and the artwork that will follow in this unit. Teachers and their students will share their strengths as a visual artist, set goals for themselves and select three artifacts to share that will demonstrate who they are as artists and how the arts are a part of their lives.

The second project—"What's the Big Idea?"—explores the big ideas in visual arts and includes How the Arts are Organized, How the Arts Communicate and How the Arts Shape and Reflect Culture. Teachers and students begin through exploring the elements and principles of art and design to develop our vocabulary or art. We will find examples of these elements and principles in our classroom environment, the natural environment, the illustrations we view and the artwork we research. Then we will discuss the art materials and techniques that we already use in creating works of art.

The third project—"Who's Art Is It?"—engages teachers and student pairs in research to learn more about How the Arts Communicate and How the Arts Shape and Reflect Culture to discover an artist (historical or contemporary), or a period in art history, or an art technique, or an art form, or the art of a specific culture to create a PowerPoint presentation to share with the class.

The fourth project—"What Do I Want To Create?"—engages teachers and students in identifying a series of art projects that they want to engage in to communicate something that is important to them in their lives. Teachers and students will identify a person, or place, or thing, or a social issue, or a concept that is important to them. Teachers and students will select the art materials and techniques that they want to use to communicate their topic with others. Teachers and students may refer to either the subject matter, the techniques or the concepts derived from their shared experiences with their art research project or the research of their peers.

The fifth project—"Where Can I Share My Artwork with Others?"—explores how artists share their work with others through art exhibitions as a means of publishing their work. Teachers and students begin to conceptualize an art exhibition to share their work with their school community and their families and make decisions on how to mount and display their finished work.

The sixth project and culminating event in this unit—"Will You Come to Our Art Opening?"—is the art exhibition and opening reception where students can share their work with others. The process of organizing and preparing this event becomes an important part of the curriculum when students are engaged in the entire process from developing a guest list, to designing invitations, to preparing a menu, to creating the program of events and hosting the event.

This unit models highly effective practices in visual arts education. Through the experiences in this unit teachers, children and youth are empowered through the four major disciplines in the arts including, art history, art production, art criticism and aesthetics while creating, performing and responding to their own work and the work of professional artists.

National Standards in the Visual Arts

The National Standards in the Visual Arts that are met through the work in this unit are:

Content Standard I
Understanding and applying media, techniques and processes

Achievement Standard:
Kindergarten to Grade Four
· Students know the differences between materials, techniques, and processes

· Students describe how different materials, techniques, and processes cause different responses
· Students use different media, techniques, and processes to communicate ideas, experiences, and stories
· Students use art materials and tools in a safe and responsible manner

Grade Five to Grade Eight
· Students select media, techniques, and processes; analyze what makes them effective or not effective in communicating ideas; and reflect upon the effectiveness of their choices
· Students intentionally take advantage of the qualities and characteristics of art media, techniques, and processes to enhance communication of their experiences and ideas

Content Standard 5
Reflecting upon and assessing the characteristics and merits of their work and the work of others

Achievement Standard:
Kindergarten to Grade Four
· Students understand there are various purposes for creating works of visual art
· Students describe how people's experiences influence the development of specific artworks
· Students understand there are different responses to specific artworks

Grade Five to Grade Eight
· Students compare multiple purposes for creating works of art
· Students analyze contemporary and historic meanings in specific artworks through cultural and aesthetic inquiry
· Students describe and compare a variety of individual responses to their own artworks and to artworks from various eras and cultures

172

The Art Projects

Project One:
Who Am I As An Artist and How Are the Arts A Part Of My Life?[1]

This experience begins with a community building activity and is designed to help you understand the role of the visual arts in your life, identify your strengths as a visual artist, set goals for yourself as a visual artist and select three artifacts that reflect your previous experiences in the visual arts. Recording this information on your reflection guide will help you prepare for your oral presentation to the class. Sharing this information in an oral presentation will help us to get to know more about each other as visual artists and how the arts are a part of our everyday lives. The reflection guide will help you to identify

· Your strengths as a visual artist
· Three goals you are setting for yourself as a visual artist
· Steps you can take to achieve the goals you are setting for yourself
· A description of three artifacts that demonstrate something important about the visual arts in your life. In the description of the item, you will include
o why you chose the item
o what the item tells about you as an artist or about how the arts are a part of your life

Community Building Activity—Name Game
The students will—
· Form a circle outside, say names quickly to a four beat count, around in a circle, go around twice.
· Add an adjective to your name (use alliteration) that begins with the same letter as your name; go around once or twice as needed.
· Add expressive movement to name, go around once
· Say the person's name next to you and do their movement, then do your own name and movement, go around once.

The teacher will—
· Prepare the room for forming a large circle or find a place outside to work.

· Model each part of this game for the students

Exploring Line with Cursive Writing
The students will—
· Apply what they learned about alliteration and line to create a name card that explores line.
· Write their name with alliteration in cursive writing (Joyful Jennifer).
· Continue the line in their writing to explore a variety of lines to fill the page.

The teacher will—
· Prepare art materials.
· Model the project with a sample.

Reflecting on the Art Production Experience
The students will—
· Reflect on the art experiences by creating a title for the experience, listing the materials, reflecting on their personal involvement in the art process, taking a photograph of their artwork, placing the documentation in their portfolio.

The teacher will—
· Prepare the reflection template for each student

Who Am I As An Artist and How are the Arts a Part of My Life?
The students will—
· Identify their strengths as a visual artist.
· Establish three goals for themselves as a visual artist.
· Describe steps you can take to achieve the goals you are setting for yourself.
· Describe three artifacts that demonstrate something import about the visual arts in your life and why you chose the artifact and what it tells about you as an artist or how the arts are a part of your life.

The teacher will—
· Send a letter home to describe the project.
· Prepare a reflection guide for the students that is developmentally appropriate.

· Share his/her own project with the students and include all of the components of the project.

· Lead students in developing their reflection guide.

· Develop a strategy for the oral presentations that allows two to three students to each make at 5-minute presentation each in one sitting.

Modifications for kindergarten students who will—

· Write letters of their name and use words to describe the types of lines in the letters (i.e. curved line, straight line, diagonal line, combination curved and straight line, etc.).

· Bring one item they made to share with the class.

· Describe why they are an artist and the item with the sentence starter, "I am an artist because I made _____." (i.e. this bracelet for my mom, this painting of my dog, this lego toy, this sandcastle with my friend, this snowman with my sister, etc.).

· Set one goal such as, "This year I want to learn to _____."

The teacher of kindergarten students will—

· Send a letter home to families describing the project.

· Prepare and review sentence starters on chart paper.

· Record what students say.

Project Two:
What's the Big Idea?

The second project—"What's the Big Idea?"—explores the big ideas in visual arts and includes:

· How the Arts are Organized.
· How the Arts Communicate.
· How the Arts Shape and Reflect Culture.

Teachers and students begin through exploring the elements and principles of art and design to develop our vocabulary or art. We will find examples of these ideas in our classroom environment, the natural environment, the illustrations we view and the artwork we research. Then we will discuss the art materials and techniques that we already use in creating works of art.

Focusing Event—How the Arts are Organized
The students will—
· Fold a 8 1/2" X 11" sheet of paper into eight sections.
· Label each section for an element of art and design moving from left to right.
· Line, shape, texture, form, value, space, color.
· Use a pen or a pencil to draw examples of each element.
· Reflect on the experience using the reflection guide.

The teacher will—
· Prepare the art materials needed and a sample product.
· Model each element for the students by sharing the samples.
· Prepare the refection guide.
· Model reflecting on the experience using the reflection guide.

Element and Principles Exploration
in the Built and Natural Environment
The students will—
· Identify and locate places in the classroom where they see the elements of line, shape, color and texture in the classroom.
· Identify and locate places in the natural environment where they see the elements of line, shape, color, form texture, space, value.
· Record their findings on a reflection guide.

The teacher will—
· Prepare a series of open-ended questions:
  · Where do you see line in our classroom?
  · Where do you see shape in our classroom?
  · Where do you see form in our classroom?
  · What items in our classroom do you think have texture?

Can you use:
    · a word to describe the texture you are referring to in each item?
  · What items in our room draw our attention to the element of color?
  · Prepare a reflection guide for students to record their findings.

Finding the Elements in a Work of Art
The students will—
· Identify the elements and principles of art found in teacher selected images.
· Work in teams to record evidence of the elements and principles of art and design they found in the selected artwork.

The teacher will—
· Select artwork that demonstrates a variety of elements and principles of art and design.
· Divide students into groups of three,
· Prepare a reflection guide to record the elements and principles of art and design to include the name of the artwork they were viewing.

Modifications for kindergarten students who will—
· Explore one element of art at a time by drawing on paper that is 8-1/2 X 11 inches.
· Arrange pages of the elements in the order established by the teacher.
· Find examples of each element in objects in nature or in the classroom.
· Point to areas in a reproduction that show how an artist uses line, shape, color or texture in their work.

The kindergarten teacher will—
· Prepare paper and drawing tools for elements of art.
· Create a bound book of student created art elements.
· Select objects to bring in from nature or plan a nature walk or classroom search for art elements.
· Select reproductions that are appropriate for the activity.
· Demonstrate pointing to a specific area in a reproduction to identify the use of line, shape, color or texture.
· Distribute reproductions to students and circulate around the room to check for understanding when asking students to point one area at a time where the artist used line, shape, color or texture in their work.

Project Three:
Who's Art Is It?

The first purpose of this project is to help you and your students become acquainted with well-known historical and contemporary artists, periods in art history, art techniques and the art of diverse cultures. The second purpose is to give you and your students practice describing art and developing strategies that will motivate you to look closely at works of art, think critically about what you see, and articulate what is seen. The third purpose is to create a visual such as a PowerPoint Presentation that you can share with others. The fourth purpose is to use your research and images to develop art experiences that are related to the concept, subject matter, technique, or media, and to teach skill development while connecting the art experience to the lives of children and to a thematic unit of study. It is important to note that quite often the work of practicing artists in your own community can be a powerful component to this project because in some cases the subject matter of their artwork may be more familiar to your students and may be more relevant in that it may reflect the natural environment of your region or social and cultural issues that are important to your region.

Focusing Event—
Review of Elements and Principles of Art and Design
    The students will—
    · Move into a circle using a 10 second countdown.
    · Say one thing that is on they learned about the elements and principles of art.

    The teacher will—
    · Prepare the room for making a circle.
    · Model the activity by saying one thing about the elements and principles of art.

Who's Art Is It?
    The students will—
    · Select an artist, a period in art history, an art technique, or a culture to research.

· Create a PowerPoint presentation that contains the following components—
> · Title page that describes your presentation and includes your name
> · Background information either about the artist, the period in art history, the culture, or the art technique.
> · Images of selected artwork (three or more).
> · A series of open-ended questions to get others to look closely at the art work.
> · List a series of art production experiences that you or your peer might want to engage in that will build on the art talk.

· Prepare an oral presentation that use the PowerPoint slides and the open-ended questions to engage the class in looking closely at the selected images to articulate what is seen.

· Assess their own PowerPoint and presentation using a student-created checklist that is based on the teacher's PowerPoint and presentation.

The teacher will—

· Chose a research topic to share with students.

· Prepare a PowerPoint presentation to share with the students.

· Model the expectations for the PowerPoint and the Presentation.

· Guide students in creating rubric for the PowerPoint and the Presentation for assessing their own work.

· Develop a strategy that limits the student presentations to three presentations in one sitting.

Modifications for kindergarten students who will—

· Select a reproduction of an art work that they like from printed images the teachers has made available that includes the name of the image and the title of the work.

· Tell what they think the image is about using a sentence starter such as, "I think this picture is about_____."

· Tell why they like the image using a sentence starter such as, "I like this picture or I don't like this picture because_____."

The kindergarten teacher will—
· Prepare the reproductions of images from the work of selected artists that will be interesting to young children. Include the title of the piece and the name of the artist.
· Develop a strategy for sharing these statements and limit the presentations to three children at one sitting.

Project Four:
What Do I Want To Create?

The fourth project—"What Do I Want To Create?"—engages teachers and students in identifying a series of art projects that they want to engage in to communicate something that is important to them in their lives. Teachers and students will identify a person, or place, or thing or a social issue or a concept that is important to them this year. Teachers and students will select the art materials and techniques they want to use to communicate their topic with others. Teachers and students may refer to the subject matter, the techniques or the concepts derived from your shared experiences with your own art research project or the research of your peers. The creative process may focus on a shared theme or an individual theme.

The students will—
· View the teacher's finished artwork.
· Analyze the steps in the creative process.
· Make connections to the writing process.
· Decide if they want to explore a shared theme or an individual theme.
· Engage in all aspects of the creative process to include brainstorming, selecting a theme, drawing sketches, selecting media and techniques, experimenting with media and techniques, creating a series of work to explore the theme, matting or displaying the work, reflecting on the process, sharing the finished artwork with their peers.

The teacher will—
· Model the creative process for the students.
· Engage in all aspects of the creative process to include

brainstorming, selecting a theme, drawing sketches, selecting media and techniques, experimenting with media and techniques, creating a series of work to explore the theme, matting or displaying the work, reflecting on the process, sharing the finished artwork with the students.

· Create a developmentally appropriate checklist for students to indicate where they are in the creative process.

Modifications for kindergarten students who will—
· Brainstorm a shared theme for their artwork.
· Explore individual ways to depict the subject matter selected.
· Engage in learning centers that will offer different media to depict the subject matter selected.
· Create several pieces about the subject matter.
· Select finished work to share with each other and their families.
· Create a title for their artwork.
· Describe what their artwork is about.
· Talk about the names of the materials and techniques they used.

The kindergarten teacher will—
· Help students select a subject matter for their artwork.
· Set up a variety of learning centers that offer different materials to depict the subject matter.
· Guide students in talking about their finished work.
· Provide an opportunity to share their work with their peers.

Project Five:
Where Can I Share My Art Work with Others?

The fifth project—"Where Can I Share My Art Work with Others?"—explores how artists share their work with others through art exhibitions as a means of publishing their work. Teachers and students begin to conceptualize an art exhibition to share their work with their school community and their families and make decisions on how to mount and display their finished work. A learning trip to a local art exhibition is an ideal way to begin this project where students can take notes to record the elements of an exhibition.

The students will—
· Brainstorm locations for the art exhibition.
· Select their own pieces to display in the art exhibition.
· Select a method for matting or displaying their finished work.
· Determine the finished size of their work.
· Record the information on an index card attached to their work.
· Use the self-reflection guide to document their work.

The teacher will—
· Arrange for a learning trip to visit a local art exhibition or show students a web site or photographs of an art exhibition.
· Send a letter home to ask for parent volunteers to assist with matting student work.
· Contact a frame shop or a wholesale vendor for matt board and paper tape to use for displaying artwork.
· Provide examples of ways to display artwork in an exhibition.
· Assist students in deciding how to display their work.

Modifications for kindergarten students who will—
· Visit an art exhibition in the community.
· Tell one thing they like about the art exhibition.
· View the location for the kindergarten art exhibit.
· Take a digital photograph of their artwork to show at the exhibition.

The kindergarten teacher will—
· Describe an art exhibition to the students.
· Take students to an art show in the community.
· Share the specific location for the kindergarten art exhibition.
· Guide students in taking a digital photograph of their artwork.
· Contact parent or upper grade volunteers to assist with the exhibition.

Project Six:
Will You Come to Our Art Opening?

The sixth project and culminating event in this unit—"Will You Come to Our Art Opening?"—is the art exhibition and opening reception where students can share their work with others. The process of organizing and preparing this event becomes an important part of the curriculum when students are engaged in the entire process from developing a guest list, to preparing invitations, to preparing a menu, to developing the program of events and hosting the event.

The students will—
· Volunteer for a role and responsibility to make the art opening a success.
· Event coordinator for overall concept of the event and activities.
· Exhibition designer to plan the layout of the show.
· Exhibition installation to hang the artwork and artists' statements.
· Program planning for the order of the events.
· Public relations officer for announcing the event in the right places.
· Graphic designer for designing invitations and advertising the event.
· Photocopier for making copies of the invitations and flyers for the event.
· Calligrapher for addressing invitations.
· Menu planning for the reception.
· Catering for making and presenting the food at the reception.
· Serving the food during the reception.
· Host and hostess during the event to welcome guests.
· Speakers at the event for welcoming, introduction, overview of the project.
· PowerPoint presenters at the event to share the research of several students.
· Room set up for the reception.
· Photographer for documenting the event.
· Room clean up after the opening.
· Reporter for the event.

The teacher will—
· Define the developmentally appropriate roles for students to

contribute to the process of planning the art opening and reception that is based on student strengths and student partners that will work well together.

Modifications for kindergarten students who will—
 · Create an invitation to their art show.
 · Mail the invitation to their parents.
 · Volunteer to bring a food item to the art opening.
 · Share one sentence about their artwork with their families at the art opening while a slide of their artwork is shown using a digital projector.

The kindergarten teacher will—
 · Prepare slideshow of student artwork.
 · Matt and hang student artwork in an appropriate location.
 · Ask parent volunteers or students in an upper grade level to assist with the planning and preparing the art opening.

Sample of a Self-Reflection Template for Engaging in the Art Process

Art Production Experience Reflection Guide

I can create a title for this art experience:
I can describe the motivation for creating my own work of art:
I can list the materials I used:
I can reflect on my personal involvement in the creative process during this art experience:
I can attach a photograph of my completed artwork:

Suggested Art Materials

Grumbacher Watercolor Sets
Watercolor Brushes, flat and round
10-well Plastic Paint Palettes
Tempera or Acrylic Paint, primary and secondary colors, black, white
Containers with Lids for storing paint
Oil Pastels, 12 to 48 color sets
Chalk Pastel 12 to 48 color sets
Prismacolor Colored Pencil Sets
Compressed Charcoal
Sharpie Permanent Pen, Extra-fine
Sharpie Permanent Pen, Fine
Crayons 24 to 48 color box
Acid-Free Assorted Colored Paper Pads or Bulk 12"x18"
Watercolor paper pads or bulk 11"x15"
Drawing paper pads or bulk 12"x18"
Drawing paper bulk, 24" X 36"
Drawing pencils or Draughting pencils
Pink Pearl Erasers
Kneeded Erasers, large
Elmer's Glue 8 oz bottles
Scissors
Metal and Wooden Rulers
Matt Knives
Matt Boards
Acid-free Tape

Suggested Equipment and Software

Computers
Access to the Internet
Digital Camera
Color Printer
PowerPoint Software in Microsoft Office
Printer Paper
Digital Projector
White Wall or Screen for Projector

Note

[1] The author would like to credit Dr. Kathryn Au with the idea for this project which is modified from a project implemented in her classroom that is based on discovering, "Who am I as a reader and writer and how is reading and writing a part of my life?"

Judicious Discipline
in the Classroom

Middle School Classrooms

Understanding
Our Basic Rights

From Material Originally Submitted
by Betty Powers

Objectives
1. To introduce the students to the rights they have as guaranteed in the First, Fourth, and Fourteenth Amendments.
2. To encourage the students to apply what is in the amendments to current events.

Time
45 minutes.

Materials
Copies of the First, Fourth, and Fourteenth Amendments, activity sheet, large sheet of drawing paper, highlighters, and markers or crayons.

Procedure
Divide the class into three groups. Give each group one of the amendments to study and a large piece of drawing paper. Tell students to circle words and highlight phrases that seem to be confusing. Discuss ways to resolve confusion and point out resources in the room that can be of help to them. Emphasize your discussions on problem solving that you have had in your class meetings. Make sure students remember the expectations regarding peaceful and respectful conflict resolution.

As each group discusses their amendment, circulate through the room to make sure they are following directions. Make sure they clearly understand the language and meaning of the amendments. (With older students, jigsaw learning can be employed here to allow the various groups to peer teach their information to members of other groups.)

After they have discussed the meaning of the amendment, have each group draw some aspect of it on their chart paper. Share the drawing and, the information if you have not done a jigsaw, with the class on what is in the amendment that protects them. (20-25 minutes)

Hand out newspapers to the groups and have the students find newspaper articles that deal with the amendment analyzed in their group. Each group should report to the class on the article and how it relates to the amendment they analyzed. Use the worksheet that follows for the last part of this activity.

Understanding Our Basic Rights Worksheet

Find a newspaper article or articles that address one of the following guaranteed freedoms:

Freedom of speech.
Freedom of religion.
Freedom of the press.
Freedom of peaceful assembly.
Freedom from unreasonable search and seizure.
A person cannot be denied life, liberty, or property without
    due process.
All persons are entitled to equal protection under the law.

Attach your group's article to this worksheet, then complete the following:

What happened?

What right does this involve?

Were the person's rights protected? Explain your answer.

What Are Our Responsibilities

Objectives

1. To encourage the students to evaluate their responsibilities toward each other.

2. To introduce under what conditions the students' rights give way to the majority—Compelling State Interests.

3. To have students apply their new knowledge of rights and responsibilities in given situations requiring decision making about what action should be taken.

Time

45 minutes.

Materials

Two word strips for each student, copies of the decision worksheets for each student.

Procedure

Review the rights previously presented and write them on the board or on an overhead. State that when one has rights one also has responsibilities. Pass out two word strips to each small group of students. Tell them they will use one strip to write down one of the guaranteed rights—you should assign each group a different right. On the other word strip they will write down a responsibility that goes with the right.

Brainstorm with them about how rights go with responsibilities. For instance, one right is freedom of the press; The corresponding responsibility would be to report accurately, don't lie.

Give students a few minutes to complete this activity and then have them post their strips on a bulletin board.

Introduce the concept that on specific occasions a student's rights may be lost if they are not exercised responsibly. Rights can be lost when the state, or in this case a teacher, can show a Compelling State Interest. The Compelling State Interests are: Property loss and damage; Legitimate Educational Purpose; Health and Safety; and Serious Disruption of the Educational Process. Write them on the board, and have the students brainstorm examples of situations that might involve the four interests. For instance, we have speed limits and stop signs for the sake of health and safety.

Talk about how these same compelling interests can be used for classroom rules. In small groups have students brainstorm four rules, one for each of the interests. Post the rules. Are there any significant differences between the lists? Discuss the differences, if any, and reach consensus on what the four classroom rules will be. (Remember to help students use positive and respectful language in their rules.)

Extended Activity

Have the class break up into small groups. Give each group copies of Worksheet Three, "What Are The Issues?" Have them come up with one or more possible solutions to the problems presented.

Closure

Review the rules you have agreed on. Let students know you will be having class meetings and those will be opportunities to discuss when rules are working and not working.

Rights and Responsibilities Worksheet

What Are the Issues?

You are a Supreme Court judge. What decision would you give? What would be your explanation? What are the issues?

1. The Constitution gives us freedom of speech. During a speech people in the audience start to heckle the person talking. They become so loud that no one can hear the speaker. What are the rights of: the hecklers, the speaker, the rest of the audience? What are the issues?

2. Two students in a class start rumors about another student in class. When confronted, they say their freedom of speech allows them to spread the rumors, whether or not they are true. What are the issues?

3. The Constitution guarantees freedom of the press. Students complain that some of their newspaper articles are being censored or severely edited. They say this violates their rights. What are the issues?

4. A student wears a shirt to school with offensive language on it. A school official asks the student to take it off. The student says that wearing the shirt is a protected right. What are the issues?

Point of View/
Conflict Resolution

This lesson plan, which accompanies the dual picture of the old and young women on the following page, was developed as experimental material by the School Initiatives Program operating in conjunction with the Community Board Center for Policy and Training in San Francisco, California. It is reprinted here with their permission.

Age Group
    3rd through 6th grade.

Objectives
    To promote awareness of how perceptual limitations can affect communication. To promote acceptance of divergent points of view.

Time
    10 to 15 minutes.

Materials
    Transparency of young girl/old woman drawing and/or one copy for each student.

Procedure

Show picture of young girl/old woman to the group. Ask students to describe what they see in the picture. Assist students who have difficulty identifying both aspects of the drawing. [Editor's note: I have found it useful to have students trace both faces on the picture for other students who can see only one of the faces.] Expand the discussion to other areas in which a person's point of view might be limited by his/her perception of information. Ask students how this activity could be useful to them in various curriculum areas.

Process Questions

Why did some people see a young woman while others saw an old woman?

Is there a "correct" way to see the picture?

Is anybody able to see both aspects simultaneously?

How might interpersonal conflicts result from individuals perceiving information differently?

How might such conflicts be resolved?

What did you feel towards those who saw the drawing the same way you did?

Towards those who saw it differently?

What did you feel when you "discovered" the other aspect of the picture?

Point of View

Integrating Mathematics
with *Judicious Discipline*

Jane Richards

(Begin introducing the concepts of Mathematics integrated with *Judicious Discipline* by using ideas from the following discussion suggestions.)

When approaching a mathematical problem that needs to be solved, before we begin making decisions, we need to look at what we're "given." Sometimes we're given information in a word problem, restrictions on a variable (e.g., if $1/x$ is a real number, x cannot equal 0), something to graph—there are a lot of possibilities. We need to think about how the givens affect the approach we choose in solving a problem. We need to think about what the problems ask us to do or find out.

Even when there seems to be an "obvious" way to go about solving it, what would happen if we make another choice? Is one decision better than another? Why? Is it faster, easier, or the only one that is mathematically valid? Suppose we get stuck, what are the options open to us? Is it better to try something and risk making a mistake or to give up? Why? Where could we go or who could we ask for help if we need it? Have other people tried to solve a similar problem? Did they find a solution? Does it make sense? Did we arrive at the same conclusions? How would we approach this type of situation next time?

Why are there rules? What mathematical "rules" can we

think of? (Properties of each operation, properties of equality, geometric properties, etc.) Suppose we applied our problem-solving skills to analyze decisions we make when we form policies for our classroom. What are our "givens?"

Family values—rules, priorities, expectations
School policies
District policies
State Education Department policies
Laws
U.S. Constitution

[Editor's Note: At this point Ms. Richards leads her students through an overview of *Judicious Discipline*.]

Mathematicians often use a flow chart to graphically show how to make decisions and what the consequences of the decisions are. (Give examples. Discuss, review, or introduce flow charts.) How could we incorporate this into making positive decisions in our classroom?

Activity

Engage students in brainstorming rules for the class based on the Compelling State Interests. What particular areas might require special attention?

Homework
Contribution to your grade
Timeliness of arrival to class
Completing assignments on time
Classroom behavior

Divide the class into groups and have each group devise a flow chart for a specific area that needs to be explored. Encourage students to include consequences for making decisions that are different from the ones the groups decide to choose as "best."

[Editor's Note: What follows are two possible flow charts that might be devised by students. After the flow charts is a worksheet that would apply to any flow chart developed.]

Flow Chart One:
Homework

Students create flow chart related to homework.

Flow Chart Two:
Arriving Late to Class

Students create flow chart related to arriving late to class.

Worksheet

What is the Compelling State Interest involved?

What decisions are to be made

How do the "givens" affect this process?

What do you consider the best decisions to be and why?

Do your choices match the four Compelling State Interests?

How?

Check to make sure you have considered alternatives to the option you consider to be the most appropriate and have included consequences to those decisions.

Judicious Discipline
in the Classroom

Secondary Classrooms

Judicious Discipline at the Secondary Level

Richard Neuman

What follows is a set of lesson plans that may be used for introducing rights and responsibilities at the secondary level. These lessons were designed to help students understand school district rules as set out in the handbook published by the Beaverton, Oregon, school district. The unit has applicability for implementing *Judicious Discipline* as it clarifies legal issues for secondary students.

These lessons need not be reserved for Homeroom or Social Studies. However, students would not need to have this information presented during each class period. It would be sufficient to present each lesson once, with the concepts reiterated as necessary by other faculty members. As specific concerns arise in a Chemistry lab, on the playing fields, or in a Technology class, they should be addressed by the teacher involved.

[Editor's Note: These lessons require a thorough reading of Forrest Gathercoal's *Judicious Discipline* book before you attempt to use them. The issues dealt with here are subtle; please take the time to read about them and understand them before introducing them to your students.]

It can hardly be argued that either students or teachers shed their constitutional rights to freedom of speech or expression at the schoolhouse gate...

—*Tinker v Des Moines Independent School District*, 393 U.S. 503

Public school pupils shall comply with rules for the government of such schools, pursue the prescribed course of study, use the prescribed textbooks, and submit to the teacher's authority.

—Oregon Regulations, Section 339.250

From the Beaverton School District handbook:

To the teacher:

You have been charged with teaching the Beaverton School District "Student Responsibilities and Rights" pamphlet. This should involve activities and discussions of the rights of citizens under the Constitution and their responsibilities in the public school setting. This is an opportunity for students to understand individual freedoms and learn to handle responsibilities. The balance of individual rights and the needs of the majority is at the heart of this unit.

In this unit, teachers and students will learn the language of the law and how it applies to school. The activities involve a great deal of teacher/student and student/student interaction, teaching strategies initially developed in the New American lecture, "Concept Attainment," and "Peer Practice." There is also the use of the cooperative learning strategy from "Teams/Games/Tournaments."

Related issues are grouped according to a general topic for each day. The scenarios should be the basis for discussion covering key concepts or each issue. Some could be used at the beginning of class to introduce a topic. For variety, a scenario could be used in small group discussions or for mini-debates. An emphasis on the balance between rights and responsibilities should be emphasized as should the factors involved in meeting individual rights and societal needs. Continually refer students to the key points of the amendments and Compelling State Interests.

This unit will involve you and your students in questions of responsibilities and rights. Payoffs are great; teachers and students have a solid framework for discipline and shaping classroom rules as well as an appreciation of individual differences.

Day 1
Concept Attainment Activity: Rights and Responsibilities

Teacher Instructions

In concept attainment, a concept is explained by giving examples of what something is and what it isn't. (It is important that the terms Rights and Responsibilities are not revealed to the students, but that they discern these concepts from the descriptions presented.) Have students generate a list of possible words or phrases to match descriptions as you reveal each row, one at a time. As more information is revealed, students will be better able to identify the concept you are describing.

Rights

1. Guaranteed by Bill of Rights
2. Your freedoms
3. Ability to enjoy life, liberty, property
4. Something you may do.

1. No one can take away
2. Cannot be voted on
3. Not always what the majority thinks is right
4. Not what you have to do

Responsibilities

1. Helps people get along
2. Helps maintain order
3. Something you should do

1. Not always doing what you want
2. Someone will expect you to do
3. You may be punished for not doing

Day 2
Your Rights: A New American Lecture (Organizer)

The Framework
U.S. Constitution:
—law of the land
Bill of Rights:
—first 10 amendments
—cannot be voted on
Other Amendments
Freedom:
—individual vs group
Justice:
—fairness
—due process
Equality:
—distributing burdens and benefits

First Amendment
Religion:
—state cannot establish
—state cannot prohibit
Free Speech:
—spoken/written word
—dress
—length of hair
Press:
—publication and distribution on school property
Assembly

Fourth Amendment
Search and Seizure:
—against unreasonable searches
—what is reasonable

Fourteenth Amendment
Life
Property:
—all one owns

208

Liberty:
> —present to future

Due Process:
> —life, liberty, and property cannot be denied without due
>> process
> —Substantive due process:
>> —fair laws
> —Procedural due process:
>> —notice
>> —fair hearing
>> —appeal

Equal Protection:
> —sex
> —race
> —national origin
> —handicapped
> —marital status
> —age
> —religion

Activity for Day 2

Teacher Instructions

Have students copy your writing from the board/overhead to the organizer as you lecture and explain. After each heading has been discussed, have students complete the following tasks, writing their responses on the back of the organizer. The tasks may be completed by working in groups.

The Framework

    1. List names for "law of land" and where liberties are found?

    2. What three things does the Bill of Rights guarantee?

First Amendment

    1. List four freedoms.

    2. Give an example of each.

    3. Share with a neighbor.

Fourth Amendment

    1. How is this amendment like the First Amendment?

Fourteenth Amendment

    1. Define substantive and procedural due process.

    2. How are your rights like the rules of a baseball game?

Day 3
Your Responsibilities: Compelling State Interests

Rules and regulations are needed to provide structure and organization in schools. List at least 10 rules a teacher or principal has written that you have been asked to follow. Share these with a neighbor and then we will list them on the board.

1.

2.

3.

4.

5.

6.

7.

8.

9.

10.

How do you feel about these? Were they necessary? Were they fair?

Rules shouldn't just exist because someone thinks they should; rather they must have a purpose. Educators can prohibit conduct which is detrimental or harmful to the operation of schools when it can be demonstrated that there is a Compelling State Interest to do so.

There are four Compelling State Interests listed in the columns on the next page. We will discuss these. and then you can determine which of the ten rules you listed above fit into which column.

(Note to teachers: After explanation, model by putting one example in each column on a duplicate of the chart found on the next page. Duplicate the chart on an overhead or on poster board. Then have students continue to work in groups. After they understand which rules fit into this pattern and which do not, have them create class rules, one for each of the Compelling State Interests. Come together as a class to put the rules up on butcher paper for a class display.)

Compelling State Interests

   Property Loss and Damage

   Legitimate Educational Purpose

   Health and Safety

   Serious Disruption

[Editor's note—The lesson plans that follow are all designed for small group work. The basis of the activities will be to have students work together to answer:

   · What rights do the students have in the following situations?
   · Which Compelling State Interests are involved?
   · Which way should the balance tip—in favor of the students or the public school?
Be ready to explain your answers.]

Day 4
Attendance and Enrollment

Key Words/Concepts
> compulsory
> exceptions—the impact of family values
> attendance in designated school
> educational alternatives

Scenarios

1. John doesn't want to attend the designated school in his area.

2. The Smiths do not want their children taking a sex education course.

3. John and Mary Jones want their child to attend a private school.

4. Cynthia is not given credit for a course because she missed fifteen class periods.

In groups, have the students discuss the scenarios. What rights do the students have in these situations? What are the Compelling State Interests? Which way should the balance tip—in favor of the student or the public school? These questions should be used for this activity and each subsequent activity in this unit.

Day 5
Equality of Opportunity

Key Words/Concepts
Fourteenth Amendment
discrimination
handicaps
grievance procedures

Scenarios
1. In seventh grade, boys who register for applied arts take Wood Shop while girls who register for the same course take Home Economics.
2. In Mr. Brown's class, girls may go to the lavatory without asking for permission, but boys need a hall pass to go.
3. John, a blind student, is not allowed to take shop because he might injure himself.
4. Mrs. White has her three students from Vietnam sit together so that they can help each other.
5. John, a student, got married over spring vacation. The principal of John's school has decided that John must drop out to support his wife.
6. Mr. Green, the counselor, suggested Martha take an English elective instead of math because she'd be the only girl is the class.

Use the questions from the previous activity to respond to the above scenarios.

Day 6
Classroom Behavior

Key Words/Concepts

positive academic environment
serious disruption to the educational process
plagiarism
appropriate disciplinary action

(refer back to list of rules)

Scenarios

1. Jeff complains when Mr. King asks him to stop talking during a reading period.

2. Joe is sent to the hallway when Megan complains that he is bothering her.

3. For chewing gum, Jane must stay after school for three consecutive afternoons.

4. Ms. Jones requires Sarah to take a test again when she is caught cheating.

5. For being tardy ten times, Sam's grade is lowered.

6. Jason hasn't brought a pencil to class for the fifth time and is given an "F" on the day's test.

Day 7
Student Dress and Grooming

Key Words/Concepts
First Amendment
dress code
health and safety
serious disruption of the educational process
property loss and damage

Scenarios
1. Joe is upset because he lost his shop safety glasses and Mr. Smith, his shop teacher, won't let him operate the power machinery.

2. Ms. Atkins, the principal, has announced a school-wide policy of "no hats."

3. Short skirts are prohibited from all school functions.

4. All high school boys are required to be clean-shaven.

5. Jane doesn't like the blue graduation gowns and decides to wear a red one instead.

6. Adam gets angry when he is told by a teacher that he must wear gym shoes on the gym floor.

Day 8
Search and Seizure

Key Words/Concepts
Fourth Amendment
seizure
expectancy of privacy
probable cause
health and safety emergency
a search related in scope to the circumstance
blanket search
strip search
illegal act
injurious

Scenarios
1. The principal searches a student's locker without permission after a teacher reports hearing that drugs might be in there.

2. At the end of the semester, the librarian opens all lockers looking for overdue books. Students have not been notified that the search would occur.

3. When Ms. Tucker discovers a book is missing, she searches all students individually before allowing them to leave the room.

4. A bomb threat has been phoned to the school; all lockers are opened and inspected.

5. All students are asked to empty their pockets and show the contents of all sacks and bags as they enter on the last day of school.

6. The principal suspects Joe has drugs inside his clothes and conducts a strip search.

7. The principal suspects a student has cigarettes inside her purse, but she refuses to let him search for them. The principal calls the student's parents who give permission for the search.

Day 9
Suspension and Expulsion

Key Words/Concepts
   suspension
   expulsion
   procedural due process
   substantive due process
   fair hearing
   counsel
   cross examination
   prognosis for rehabilitation

Scenarios

1. The vice-principal sends Sally to in-school suspension for two days. She decides not to tell her parents.

2. Don is suspended until his parents come in for a conference.

3. Marlene is suspended for having cigarettes at the school dance.

4. In December the vice-principal suspends a student for the rest of the school year.

5. John will not graduate because he has been expelled and cannot attend classes.

6. Jason's parents requested a hearing and the hearings officer decide to expel Jason. Jason's parents don't like the decision.

Day 10
Freedom of Expression

Key Words/Concepts
 libel
 slander
 pervasive vulgarity
 Federal Equal Access Act
 procedural due process
 insubordination
 public display of affection
 time, place, manner
 tolerance
 prior restraint

Scenarios
 1. A teacher tells a student that she won't be allowed to give her oral report on "How Communism Has Helped China."
 2. Jane is given detention because she called her teacher a "bitch."
 3. Frank and Sally are suspended from school because they were kissing in the hallway.
 4. Tom is asked to remove his "Nixon for President" button.
 5. A teacher is asked to remove a political button.
 6. The principal tells the newspaper staff they may not print the article criticizing the school lunches.
 7. Johnny is told to stop passing out anti-abortion pamphlets in his classes.
 8. The "Youth for Hitler" group is not allowed to use school facilities before, during, or after school.

Day 11
Privileged and Confidential Communication

Key Words/Concepts
   confidentiality
   Family Education Rights and Privacy Act
   professional ethics
   professional "need to know"
   criminal activity

Scenarios

1. Diane tells her counselor she can't get along with her parents. The counselor calls the home to find out what's wrong.

2. Bob tells his counselor that he is being ridiculed in class by his science teacher. The counselor speaks to the teacher to hear the other side of the story.

3. Jane tells her P.E. teacher she has been beaten by one of her parents. The teacher calls law enforcement.

4. Joe tells a teacher that he shoplifted some school supplies. The teacher calls the store and sets up an appointment for Joe to meet with the manager.

5. A teacher posts the grades of all students in her classroom to help them identify their missing assignments.

Day 12
Student Records

Key Words/Concepts
  Family Educational Rights and Privacy Act
  accurate information

Scenarios
  1. Johnny, a ninth grader, thinks Mr. Williams, the P.E. teacher, put some negative remarks in his file. He is told he can't see the records.

  2. His parents ask to see the file and, after reviewing the contents, state that they don't agree with Mr. Williams' comments about Johnny being "lazy" and "a goof-off."

Additional Activities/Resources
for the Secondary Classroom

1. Peer Practice

To assist in the learning and understanding of key words and concepts, the strategy of peer tutoring can be used. In this activity, students help each other learn and practice the meanings of terms. It would be best used when an issue has a great number of new words or concepts to associated with it, i.e., freedom of expression.

The teacher needs to prepare two handouts for each pair of students. Each has two columns. Handout A has a list of half of the lesson's terms for the first student to define or explain. The correct definitions are in the right column of Handout B, which the other student holds. Along with the definitions are hints to help the "tutoring" student "tutor" the learner. After going through both sets of terms, papers can be exchanged and repeated.

2. Teams/Games/Tournaments

This activity was developed at Johns Hopkins University as a cooperative learning strategy. Students are divided into *study* groups of four; each group is balanced by sex and ability. Students help each other within this study group to learn a list of 20 to 25 key words concepts.

Study groups then go out to "compete" in a tournament. For the tournament, students are reorganized at tables according to *ability*. Different questions regarding the key words and concepts are chosen at random and asked in turn around the table. A correct answer earns a point for the answering student.

After the tournament, individual points are added for a *study group* total. Rewards are given to the winning groups although each group may win by meeting a previously established criteria for winning (i.e., 20 points out of a possible 25 points.)

3. Poster Project

Once the constitutional amendments have been studied, groups should choose one each to display on a poster. Words and illustrations should show an understanding and interpretation of the amendments. Posters should be posted, with student permission, for frequent reference.

4. Letter Writing

Encourage students to write appropriate school or government officials to ask questions or express opinions about rules, laws, or rights.

5. Writing of Class Rules

A study of rights and responsibilities leads naturally into the writing of rules appropriate for a particular classroom. Start with the Compelling State Interests and then write rules that are compatible in a positive, rather than negative form. ("Be polite" rather than "Don't talk.") Discuss suitable consequences.

6. Visual Aid

A poster depicting blind justice holding a balance is an example of a useful visual aid. On one side are many students representing the "majority." On the other side is one lone student, representing the individual. The Compelling State Interests may be added to the "majority" side as they are studied; the amendments may be added to the individual side.

7. Guest Speakers

Invite speakers into the classroom. Possibilities include school officials such as the principal, vice-principal, or superintendent; law enforcement officers; lawyers or judges; members of minority groups to discuss discrimination; someone who has gone to school in a different country; or adults who might speak about going to school in the "good old days."

8. Written Test

If a final test is used to help evaluate learning, a balance should be found between questions covering rights and those concerning responsibilities. Too often a test on this booklet evaluates students' knowledge of specific rules rather than the concepts of why the rules exist and how they help ensure students' responsibilities and rights. An effort should be made to design questions that will allow students to analyze scenarios, and apply the information to new situations.

English as a Second Language: Two Worksheets

Juanita Weber-Shirk

Worksheet One

Which individual right is illustrated in each of the following examples?

1. When Sisavath is giving a report about Laos, the teacher tells him not to say anything good about the communist government.

2. When Thanh gets a message that some more of her family have left Vietnam by boat, the teacher asks the class to stop their work and pray for the safety of Thanh's family.

3. The students from Ms. Dwyer's class decide to study together for a large unit test. They meet after school in the park across from the public library. They have been studying for about one half hour, causing no disruptions, when a policeman tells them that they must go somewhere else to work.

4. A new student gets involved in a fight and is suspended immediately. She doesn't get a chance to explain what happened, or to ask that the suspension be dropped.

5. Luis cannot see the chalkboard from his seat in the back of the classroom. He gets a bad grade on a quiz because he could not read the questions on the board and the teacher told him not to move out of his seat one more time.

6. Mrs. Weber-Shirk cannot find her keys. She asks every student to open his or her backpack and she looks in all of them for her keys.

Worksheet Two

Which Compelling State Interest is illustrated in each of the following examples?

1. Ms. Clark will not let students jump through the windows into the courtyard. She makes them go out through the door.

2. Ms. White requires students to return the Global Studies textbooks at the end of the school year.

3. In the middle of a unit on sea life, the students ask to see the movie *Teenage Mutant Ninja Turtles*. Ms. Dwyer turns down the request.

4. Students must get certain immunizations and vaccinations in order to stay in school.

5. Ms. White does not permit students to wear headsets while she lectures.

6. Ms. Weber-Shirk will not let students write on desks or walls in her classroom.

7. Students walking in the hallways during the time classes are in session are required to be quiet.

Judicious Discipline
in the Classroom

K through 12 Classrooms

Introducing Class Meetings

Barbara Landau

For Grades K-12
(Language and seating arrangements will vary depending on the age of students, but the concepts and rules will not change.)

Objective
Students will learn that class meetings are the way to discuss a variety of issues and resolve conflicts. Students will learn/ increase their communication and mediation skills. Students will learn to consistently follow the class meeting guidelines. Students will understand how to contribute topics to the class meetings. Students will understand the time, place and manner for calling class meetings.

Materials
Poster paper and markers to record the rules for the class meetings, journals and pencils for goal setting and a white board or laminated poster or suggestion box for students to add their agenda items.

Activity
Gather students together in a circle. You can seat them on the carpet or have them circle their desks but they should be seated facing each other in a different arrangement that makes it clear

231

they are engaging in something other than a typical classroom learning activity.

Remind students that their classroom rules are based on the balance of their individual rights and their responsibilities to themselves and others. Explain that there will always be problems when things get tense or someone is having a bad day and that class meetings will be used to solve the problems in open and respectful discussions.

Tell students there are some rules that will apply to all meetings.

1. We will always sit facing each other.

2. We will always use respectful language.

3. We will never talk about students, instead we will talk about issues. In other words if someone is pushing into the front of the line, we will talk about how to line up in ways that are safe and appropriate. We will not talk about the student who pushed.

4. Students can "pass." No one has to participate in the meetings but everyone is expected to join the circle and listen. No one has to speak.

5. Class meetings will stay on topic. This is not the time to tell unrelated stories.

6. The teacher or a designated leader will conduct the meetings.

(Depending on the age of the students, this might be all you do during the first meeting.)

Part II (If Working with Younger Students)

After establishing the ground rules, discuss procedures. How often should the class meetings be held? (In elementary classrooms, some teachers begin each day with a meeting. At the intermediate, middle and high schools some teachers hold a meeting a week or once every two weeks. Meetings are important and need to be held on a regular basis in order to be effective.

You should work with your students to determine the schedule that will best suit your classroom.)

These are additional topics that are important for the class meeting process to be effective.

· What if an emergency meeting is needed?

· Who can call meetings?

· What will the topics be? (This is when you can introduce the white board or laminated poster or suggestion box. Students will put their suggested topics on or in whichever of these you decide to use.)

· Let students know you want their honest input and will make the changes you can based on their discussions.

· Talk about the purpose of the journals and how they will be used for goal setting.

(For details on class meeting guidelines, please see the chapter by Paul Gathercoal on pages 77-92.)

Developing Tolerance

Barbara Landau

*Originally Titled Ethics, This Lesson Plan Was Developed from Ideas
Contributed by Margaret Abbott*

Tolerance and Personal Responsibility

Age Group
Adaptable for 1st through 12th grade.

Objective
To stimulate awareness of individual responsibility toward
other students, learning, and the school environment.

Time
These lessons can be divided into two 30-minute sessions for
younger students or can be presented as one 45-minute session
for older students.

Materials
Chart paper, crayons, scissors, construction or drawing paper, butcher paper, felt pens.

Procedure
Ask students to think of ways they are responsible for
themselves. If they are hesitant, ask them prompts such as: "Do
you do chores at home?" "Do you have a special routine to get
ready for bed?" "Do you have responsibilities before you come to
school?"

235

Focus them on responsibilities related to school and learning by asking what students should take responsibility for when working or playing with other students in their classroom, on the playground or anywhere on school grounds. Ask them what they should be responsible for coming to or going home from school. Add all responses to the chart. Let students know they will be working with the chart tomorrow. (If working with older students, you can move on to session two right away if time allows.)

(If working with younger children, this should be the end of the first 30-minute session).

Session 2

(If breaking lesson into two sessions for younger children; otherwise procedures below should be continuation of procedures above as part of a single lesson).

Procedure

Divide students into small groups and give each group a graphic organizer divided into five columns. The columns should be headed: Learning, Playing, Keeping the Classroom Neat, Coming to School, Going Home from School. Review the chart with your students and number each item as you read it. In their groups, have students place the corresponding number for each item in the column where they think it belongs. Tell them they can put the number in more than one column if they think that is appropriate. Model the process of deciding where a number might go by using an overhead of the graphic organizer and thinking out loud about one or two of the items. Ask for student input as you model the process.

Ask the students to go through the rest of the items, placing the corresponding numbers where they think they should be. Collect the organizers and review them before the next class meeting.

Session Three

At the next class meeting spread the organizers out on the floor in the center of the circle or post them on a poster board at the side of the circle if students are sitting in desks in addition to the original chart. Look at the organizers. Did all the groups put the same numbers in the same columns? Where were there differences? Make the differences the topic of that meeting. Do the differences matter? Could the differences be the source of conflict in the future? Is there a way to sort this out? Do all groups have to agree?

Remember, you are teaching tolerance in this lesson. The primary objective for this discussion is to examine how we handle differences of opinion and value the input of others. Is there a right way to think about some of these items? Is there a wrong way? After the discussion, give your students time for a journal entry related to what you have discussed. Have them set a goal for how they will respond to differences of opinion.

Activities To Promote
Media Literacy

Donna Grace

[Ed. Note—As the author mentions below, these activities can be adapted for Grades 3 through 12]

Most media literacy curricula address (1) one's relationship with the media, (2) the conventions of production, (3) the ways in which the media shape their fare, and (4) critical/ideological aspects of the media (Desmond, 1997). Below I share some preliminary activities to use in media education based on these categories. In accordance with the principles of *Judicious Discipline*, however, some ground rules and boundaries need to be developed with the students. Inevitably, in media literacy projects, popular culture will find its way into the classroom. Students will incorporate aspects of the music, films, DVDs, etc. that they enjoy into their projects. This is to be expected and students should be allowed considerable freedom in this area. Although some aspects of popular culture may be replicated, students also have the opportunity to rework some of these images and plots in order to construct things differently in their own ways. However, limitations need to be established, particularly with regard to racism, sexism, potentially harmful stereotypes, sexual references, inappropriate or mean-spirited humor, or other objectionable words or images. As advised by Ohta (2005, p.15), "students should be involved in parameter setting and consider such things as: *How will this make different people feel? Is this really funny? And could we show it to the principal?"* This notion of audience is important. More freedom may be allowed in products made for classroom use than for those to be shared with parents, the school, or the broader community.

Keeping these things in mind, I suggest the following activities for beginning media studies. Each activity can easily be adapted for students in grades 3-12. For projects involving videotaping, small groups work best. Each group will need to decide who will fill the roles of scriptwriter(s), director, camera person, sound person (optional), and actors. Basic equipment needs include a video camera, tripod, extension cords, external microphone (if possible), and video tapes. An extra battery for the camera and external microphone should also be on hand. Tapes can be edited in-camera by rewinding and reshooting, or through the use of computer editing programs. I-movie is a particularly user-friendly program that is installed in Macintosh computers.

Photo Montage

This beginning activity is used to create awareness of one's relationship with the media, or how students use the media and how it may also use them. The intent is to demonstrate that there are positive as well as potentially negative aspects to media use. We use the media for information, entertainment, relaxation, escape, and social interaction. On the other hand, the media may influence us, for example, to make unhealthy choices in eating or lifestyle, to buy things we don't need, or portray stereotypes and unrealistic images of female beauty or masculinity.

On a large sheet of construction paper, students create a photo montage depicting the types of media that they most engage with (particular sections of newspapers, types of magazines, televisions shows, favorite movies, music, etc.).

On a sheet of notebook paper, they make two columns: Positive and Negative. Students write under each column positive and potentially negative uses/influences of the media for themselves or others.

240

The paper is attached to the montage and shared in small groups. Each group shares a summary of their positives and negatives and a class chart is compiled.

Decoding/Recoding Magazine Advertisements

Activity 1

Students work in pairs in activities 1-5 to explore how the media shape their fare. Each pair is given a different magazine ad. The students jot down thoughts about the wants, needs, or values to which the advertiser is attempting to appeal (sex appeal, snob appeal, appeal to tradition or family values, social status, romance, popularity, health, power, prestige, being cool, athletic ability, beauty, success, wealth, social class, masculinity, etc.) Wait to see what the students come up with on their own before presenting them with these appeals.

On the board or chart paper, summarize and categorize the students' responses according to the above categories.

Option: use taped television commercials to do the above with the whole group.

Activity 2

Divide the students into small groups. Pass out a different magazine ad to each small group. Have the students consider the following:

The people in the ad
The age of the people
Their expressions
Their clothing
Their body language
Their surroundings
The colors used
The camera angles used

Then have the students respond to the following questions:

What does the ad suggest about the product?
What does the ad suggest about the people using the product?

241

What techniques were used to convey this message?

Students report back to the large group and responses are summarized and categorized on the board or chart paper.

The responses are then applied to the Key Concepts of Media: Industry, Genre, Technology, Language, Audience, and Representation (see above).

Option: This activity can also be done with taped TV commercials

Activity 3

In small groups, give students each a different magazine with a different focus (teens, women, males, young children, retirees, etc.). Provide each group with a handout containing a chart with the following headings:

Product advertised
Company selling the product
Target audience
Appeal used (see activity 1)

When finished filling in the chart, students determine the most common types of ads used in the different magazines, who their target audience is, and what appeals are most often used. Results are shared with the large group.

Activity 4

Divide students into small groups.

Select magazine ads (those advertising cigarettes, liquor or junk food are good for this) and cut off the caption before making copies.

Give each group an ad and have them write their own caption "talking back" to the ad or parodying it. Share results.

Activity 5

Divide students into small groups.

Give each group a copy of a magazine ad aimed a particular group of people (males, females, children, retirees, teens).

Each group then develops a new ad using the same product for a different group of people. For example, students take an ad with a product aimed at women and change it to market the same product to men—or take an ad selling a product for babies and re-frame the product for teens. Share results.

Activity 6

The conventions of production are the focus of activities 6 and 7. Divide students into groups of 5 or 6. Give each group a different product they may not have seen before (unusual food, health or beauty products work well for this).

Have each group plan a television commercial advertising this product.

Each group needs to decide:

> The audience they want to target
> The desires they will appeal to (see above)
> How they will convey their message
> What persuasive techniques they will use

They also need to include a *brand name*, a *slogan* (catchy phrase or saying that gives an identity to the product) and *the copy* (a few sentences that describe the product and make it appealing).

The groups make or bring in props, and rehearse.

Students video tape their ad (optional) and present to the class.

Activity 7

Students learn about the genre of parody by reworking an ad to humorously expose questionable promotional strategies. For instance, the students might turn an ad for the *Fly-High Helicopter* toy that did not work as promoted into the *Fall and Flop Helicopter* toy; or the *Fit and Heart-Happy* cereal into the *Fat and Heart-harmful* cereal after reading the ingredients and nutritional information on the box; or turn *Beach-time Barbie* into *Anorexic Barbie* focusing on unrealistic body images for females. Students can parody the titles, the promotional information provided, and/or the products themselves (see Ohta, 2006, at www.hawaii.edu/ed/edper/). The students script, rehearse, and video-tape (optional) and present their ad parody to the class.

Activity 8

In this activity, students address the critical/ideological aspects of the media as they critique a children's television show or movie for stereotypes (Beauty and the Beast, Cinderella, Snow White, and Lilo and Stitch work well).

Begin by giving students a chart with the following headings: females, males, characters of color, the elderly, the overweight (you may think of other categories to add after previewing the film). Tell the students that animals and personified objects can fill these categories as well as people.

Have students watch a segment of the film or pre-selected clips and jot down the roles the characters play and how they are portrayed. Have them think about who plays the lead? the buffoon? the servant? What do the characters want out of life? What do women other than the main character do in the film? How are people of color portrayed? (adapted from Christensen, 1994).

Option: this activity can also be done with picture books.

Additional Media Projects

Research a community issue and make a video documentary, including interviews representing multiple perspectives on the topic.

Create and videotape a public service announcement that can be presented to the school, community, or aired through the public access television station.

Script, storyboard, and videotape collaboratively developed student stories.

Produce and videotape a classroom or school news show.

Create a class or school newspaper, magazine, or comic book.

Develop a music video or video poetry.

Produce and video tape a class cooking show, involving students in the use of math and measurements. The tape can be shared with other classes.

Critique a sitcom or other television show aimed at a younger group of viewers.

Useful Websites

1. Media for Media Literacy (resources, reading room, best practices). http://medialit.org

2. Center for Media Education-Children and the Media. Http://www.cme.org/children/index_chld.html

3. Challenge 2000 Multilmedia Project (lesson plans): http://pblmm.k12.ca.us/PBLGuide/Activities/Activities.html#medialit

4. Just Think Foundation (curricula, resources): http://www.justthink.org/index.html

5. Youth Learn (activities, resources). http://www.youthlearn.org/learning/activities/multimedia/medialit.asp

Part Three

Building Judicious Communities

Part Three

Providing Staff Instruction in *Judicious Discipline*

Barbara Landau

The lesson plans that follow were initially developed by Dawn Pierce for use with school bus drivers in the Harpursville, New York, School District. The concepts have here been adapted to assist in the in-service training of all school support staff.

Session One:
Responsibilities of Support Personnel

Objective

To review and discuss the compelling state interests and how they relate to the responsibilities of school support personnel.

Materials

Chart paper, markers, paper, pencils, and name tags.

Procedure

1. Explain to staff members that the purpose of the workshop is to help them work more effectively with students in a variety of situations. Discuss the idea that education occurs throughout the school setting and everyone in the school plays a role in helping children understand their citizenship responsibilities. Remind them that they are part of the educational team. They can enhance the learning environment through their modeling and instruction.

2. Ask the staff members to break up into small groups. Choose one person to record on a sheet of poster paper what their group discusses concerning staff responsibilities. Their task is to:

a. Identify the roles present in their group. Are they bus drivers, secretaries, etc?

b. Each group member should state what his or her assigned responsibilities include.

c. How do they see their roles contributing to a school-wide management plan?

3. Ask the small groups to post their lists around the room when they are finished. As groups finish, ask all members of the workshop to review the information on all the sheets of paper and with a marker, put a check next to any statement that reflects their contribution to the school-wide management plan. Explain to them that assigned duties do not matter. They should check anything that seems to fit what they do on a day-to-day basis.

While some contributions will be very specific to the positions each member holds, many will overlap. When everyone has had a chance to look at the sheets and check off the contributions, the workshop leader should list on a separate sheet of poster paper those items that received the most checkmarks. Some items will be duplicated and only need to be copied once.

Emphasize the shared responsibilities even though the positions are different. A safe, productive and equitable learning community depends on common goals and shared responsibilities. The task completed will show what all of these people have in common rather than the ways their positions are different. It will help them to understand they are part of a larger community rather than an isolated member.

4. Review the list compiled by the workshop leader and ask if anything else should be added. Are there things that should be deleted?

5. Review the Compelling State Interests and how the language of the four interests is being or has been used to develop school-wide rules.

6. Ask participants to gather again in their small groups. Using the compiled list of responsibilities, ask the groups to assign each of their responsibilities to a Compelling State Interest. Each group should record its work on another sheet of poster paper.

7. When they are done with this, ask them to post the new lists around the room.

8. As a whole group, look at the lists. Which compelling interest has the most items under it? (This will probably be health and safety.) Which has the least? (This will probably be Legitimate Educational Purpose.) Emphasize that their primary shared responsibility is the safety of the students. They each play an important role in helping the school to be a safe place for students to learn. Tell them that *Judicious Discipline* places responsibility for safe behavior on students. All the adult members of the learning community are responsible for helping students learn how to act in ways that are safe, healthy and respectful.

Thank them for their work during this session and tell them they will be working together again on management issues in the near future. Workshops should always be short, pleasant, and supportive. In this way, respect is demonstrated for the very important contributions made by staff personnel.

Session Two:
Responsibilities of Students

Objective

To review the responsibilities of the students.

Materials

Overhead of the list of responsibilities below, chart paper, markers, paper, pencils, and name tags.

Some of the Staff Responsibilities

1. Safety of the children.
2. Teaching and modeling rights and responsibilities.
3. Teaching and modeling cooperation.
4. Teaching the students correct procedures on the bus, playground, lunch line, etc.

5. Teaching the students correct emergency procedures associated with your duties.

6. Knowing your students.

7. Being fair in dealing with disciplinary problems while following school management policies.

8. Being professional at all times.

9. Greeting students cheerfully to start their day out right.

10. Being conscientious concerning public relations with parents.

Is this list comprehensive? Should some items be clarified? Should other items be added?

Procedure

1. Students need to attend schools that are physically and emotionally safe places for them to be. Staff members play a very important role in helping to maintain a safe school community.

Put up the overhead that lists responsibilities (above). Ask participants to get in small groups and answer the questions at the bottom of the overhead. Have them record their answers or further questions on the chart paper they have. When you come back as a whole group, invite participants to share their answers to the questions or their further questions by posting their papers at the front of the room. Go through their answers and questions carefully and respectfully. Make sure all their concerns have been addressed. It is very important for them to know they are supported and important members of the school safety team.

2. After this discussion, go on to explain that students also have responsibilities for maintaining a safe and healthy environment while they are on the buses, in the cafeteria, on the playground, etc.

3. Hand out the school's standing policies for behavioral expectations. If your school is in the process of developing policies based on *Judicious Discipline*, work with the policies that are being formulated. This would be an excellent opportunity for the staff to have authentic input into decisions they will be asked to implement.

4. Discuss how the behavioral expectations reflect the Compelling State Interests. If the school is developing the policies discuss how basic behavioral expectations can be matched to the Interests.

252

Session Three:
Continuing to Work on Responsibilities

1. Ask staff members to break up into small groups, with one person selected to be group recorder. Write down what the groups discusses concerning student responsibilities during the school day. Have them group the responsibilities under the appropriate Compelling State Interest.

2. After the small groups have completed this task, call them back together for a large group session. Present the concepts of commensurate and compatible consequences. Point out to staff members that it is necessary to think creatively when dealing with discipline situations. The first question should always be "What needs to be learned here?" Avoid developing blanket policies such as removing students from buses, the playground, the cafeteria, etc. This would be a good time to invite in the school counselor, if your school is fortunate enough to have one. If not, present some of the ideas in the article on Consequences that appears at the front of this book.

3. Ask them to return to their small groups and select a behavioral situation they have faced. Apply the concepts of the Compelling State Interests as well as commensurate and compatible consequences to the situation. What would be some appropriate responses/corrections? Remember, the goal is for students to learn something useful about how to avoid the problem next time. The presenter should circulate to assist the groups in developing consequences.

4. Call the participants back together to discuss the ideas each group developed. Emphasize in closing that all students share a mutual responsibility for appropriate school behavior. Every member of the faculty, staff, and administration of a school should try to work with each student to help assure a safe learning community and an equal educational opportunity for all community members.

Following is a brief listing of student responsibilities. The presenter may want to contribute some of these if the participants don't include them.

Student Responsibilities
    1. Respect the rights and needs of others.
    2. Understand that with every right there is a responsibility.

Finally, emphasize that their school has defined or is in the process of defining the Compelling State Interests in specific language. The responsibility of students is to work within those guidelines. The responsibility of faculty, staff, and administration is to help students understand the guidelines and provide appropriate information when students forget the guidelines.

Wrap-Up Session for Support Staff

Discuss the issues involved in reporting a problem. In their small groups have them answer the following questions and record their answers on chart paper.

1. Who needs to hear about the problem and who does not?

2. What would be effective ways to communicate with parents when there is a problem?

3. What is the school's chain of command for reporting an incident?

Return to the situations discussed yesterday. Invite participants to offer suggestions on how to respond to difficult situations while adhering to the spirit of *Judicious Discipline*. Encourage them to bring up other situations they have faced in the past. Make sure they understand the ways *Judicious Discipline* would apply to a wide variety of problems. Also emphasize that *Judicious Discipline* does not provide a set of responses that you always use. Rather it encourages creative problem solving and the professional use of questioning strategies for resolving concerns.

Finally, thank them for their participation. Reassure them that the whole school is developing the policies and there will inevitably be some bumps along the way. Emphasize their need to support each other and your confidence that they will be successful.

Working To Solve Problems School Wide

Editor's Introductory Note: The following pages include examples of rules and consequences developed by various schools employing *Judicious Discipline* as a school-wide management program. The teachers and administrators involved placed their emphasis management as problem solving rather than a system based on rewards and punishments.

Included in these examples are problem-solving worksheets. These worksheets can be used in a number of ways. If students need a time-out, the worksheets allow them to reflect on their behaviors and can be used to start a problem-solving conversation between a student and teacher, counselor or administrator. They should never be used as punishments or without adult input, and a one-on-one problem-solving session with the student after the worksheet has been partially or completely filled out. Some teachers encourage their students to draw the problem, an appropriate alternative for any age group.

Examples of School-Wide Rules

South Elementary School Student Management Plan
St. Peter, Minnesota

Self Discipline is our goal for all students at South Elementary. We want students to develop responsibility for themselves and their own actions. We believe that if a student infringes upon the rights of others there must be fair and consistent consequences for that action. We do not want anyone to interrupt or prevent our students from learning. We strive to teach self-discipline by reasoning, discussing alternative behavior, and attempting to deal with each problem in a fair and consistent manner. Our faculty and staff realize that everyone makes mistakes, but our goal is to help students learn from their mistakes so they are less likely to repeat them. We attempt to treat each student with the dignity and respect [each] deserve[s] during that teaching process.

Our ultimate goal is to prepare students to be contributing members of a society which uses a democratic process. It is hoped that students who leave South Elementary will possess academic and social skills that will begin to prepare them to function as responsible citizens.

Student responsibilities [are to]:
Act in a safe and healthy way.
Treat all property with respect.
Respect the rights and needs of others.
Take responsibility for learning.

General School Rules
Lacomb Elementary School, Lacomb, Oregon

1. Act in a Safe and Healthy Way
Be kind with words and actions. Use furniture and equipment appropriately, walk in the building, follow playground rules, follow lunch line rules, follow bus riding rules, keep hands and feet to self. (Compelling State Interest: Health and Safety.)

256

2. Treat All Property with Respect

Take care of school property and equipment. Respect and care for the personal property of yourself and others. Borrow property of others only after receiving permission. If you break someone's property, fix or replace it. (Compelling State Interest: Property Loss and Damage.)

3. Respect Rights and Needs

Work and play without disrupting others, show courtesy towards others, cooperate to help others learn, use positive words and actions. (Compelling State Interest: Serious Disruption of the Educational Process.)

4. Take Responsibility for Your Learning

Work hard and do your best, come to school prepared to learn, be a good listener, turn in your assignments on time, do your homework, have necessary materials, set a good example for others, feel good about yourself, be on time. (Compelling State Interest: Legitimate Educational Process.)

Time, Place and Manner

The *Time*, *Place*, and *Manner* display below can be developed into a poster to use as reminders in hallways or on bulletin boards in individual classrooms.

Time

Is this a good time for what you are doing or what you are about to do?

Place

Is this a good place for what you are doing or what you are about to do?

Manner

Is your manner appropriate for this environment?

Questions and Statements for Initiating Problem Solving

Any adult member of the school community can use these questions when he or she witnesses a student acting in an unsafe or disrespectful manner. This is not a script. What is important is to approach all discipline problems with a question first and always to consider them as teachable moments.

1. It sounds/looks like you are upset. Would you like to talk about it now? Is there a better time? I want us to be able to work this thing through.

2. What happened?

3. What should you be doing right now?

4. Where should you be right now?

5. What will I see you doing when I come back here?

6. Is there something I can do to help?

7. Does this answer look right to you?

8. Tell me what you think would be the best way to resolve this.

9. Is this a reasonable time?

10. Is this a reasonable place?

11. Is this a reasonable manner?

What To Do When A Rule Is Broken:
Possible Consequences
South Elementary School, St. Peter, Minnesota

Possible Consequences Could Include

Self-Evaluation/Conference Form
Apology
Conference with Students and/or Parents
Restitution
Redoing an Assignment
Counseling
School Service Project
Loss of Privileges
Study with a Tutor or Study-Buddy
Time Out
Problem-Solving Room
Mediation

258

Resources Available for Problem Solving
Teachers
Counselor/Social Worker
Learning Disabilities Teacher
Emotional/Behavioral Disabilities Teacher
Principal
Psychologist
Self-Evaluation/Conference Form

School-Wide Learning Plan Agreement

The Principal
I support parent involvement and student success. I promise to:
· Provide an environment that protects and ensures positive communication among the teachers, caregivers, students and all of the administrative staff including me.
· Support the teachers in their efforts to regularly provide meaningful assignments that reinforce classroom instruction and meet state and national standards.
· Maintain a respectful school environment.

The Teacher
It is important that students do the best they can every day. I promise to:
· Develop and teach activities that engage students in active, meaningful learning opportunities.
· Encourage student progress and communication with caregivers by providing regular information on class work and assessment results.
· Provide meaningful homework assignments—not busy-work—for students.
· Maintain an equitable, respectful and prepared classroom atmosphere for learning.

The Caregiver(s)
I want my child to experience success in his or her academic career. I promise to:

· Help my child arrive at school on time and ready to learn.

· Work in partnership with the school to resolve discipline concerns should they arise.

· Work with my child to establish a place and time for homework.

· Stay aware of what is being learned in the classroom, encourage the efforts of my child and provide assistance as appropriate.

· Read with my child.

· Establish an appropriate bedtime and provide a healthy diet.

The Student

I want to do my best in school and have a good experience. I promise to:

· Attend school regularly, be on time and come ready to learn.

· Have a regular study time at home.

· Eat a good breakfast before coming to school.

· Be a respectful and committed member of my learning community.

· Speak with a teacher or other adult on campus if I'm having trouble with my learning.

· Work with the adults on campus to help me resolve conflicts with my peers.

Signed by _____ Principal

_____ Teacher

_____ Caregiver(s)

_____ Student

Student Self-Evaluation Form
South Elementary School, St. Peter, Minnesota

Student _____ Date _____

Time _____ Reported by _____

Today I:

because:

I did not:
    Act in a safe and healthy way _____
    Treat all property with respect _____
    Respect the rights and needs of others _____
    Take responsibility for learning _____

I should have:

Student Signature _____

Behavior Form II

Name ———————————————— Date ——————————

Today I:

Next time I will try to:

I will help myself to remember by:

(After you fill this out, a member of our school community will speak with you about the incident. Thank you for helping us help you to resolve the problem.)

Student Signature ————————————————————

Post Conference
(Student's name) and I (Problem Solving Partner's name) spoke about the problem. The following decisions were made:

Receipt Form

Heidi Weismuller

Receipts such as the one on this page should be used with students as recognition of their property rights.

RECEIPT

from _____

for _____

Turn this receipt in at the end of the day to have your item returned.

Signed _____

Date _____

An Introductory Letter
to Caregivers

From Material Originally Submitted
by Heidi Weismuller

The following letter was developed for teachers to use in introducing *Judicious Discipline* to parents and guardians. Primary caregivers are important partners in education and should be made to feel welcome in the schools and classrooms their students attend. Culture, language, socio-economics, special needs, giftedness, or just a bad experience that a primary caregiver had with school in his or her own past can all be barriers to building partnerships with the student's personal circle of influence.

The letter below is more of an invitation than an explanation of *Judicious Discipline*. It is primarily an invitation to caregivers to attend your school's open house or to come and visit at their convenience. Please make sure to have this letter translated into the primary languages spoken by your students in their homes.

Dear Parent or Guardian,

I want to introduce myself. My name is (insert name) and I have the privilege of working with your student this year in our (name of class) grade class. My most important goal for this year is to help each student do his or her personal best academically and socially. I want all of my students to feel safe and supported and, at the end of the year, move on to their next grade feeling confident and sure of their abilities.

I will work toward my goal in a number of ways. I will design lessons that engage all of us in exciting learning opportunities. I will work with students in large and small groups as well as one-on-one to help each of them succeed. And I will be using a form of classroom management called *Judicious Discipline* that teaches personal responsibility, citizenship rights, and the balance between the two. This form of management may look a little different from ones you may have seen or experienced because the emphasis in my classroom will be placed on helping children solve problems peacefully and correct problems in ways that help them learn from their mistakes. There will be consequences for inappropriate behavior but there will not be punishment.

I would very much enjoy a chance to meet with you and share the curriculum and management plans I have for this year. I invite you to attend our school's open house on _____ at _____. If you cannot attend, please call me at _____ or email me at _____ and let me know when you might be able to visit our classroom. You are always welcome to come and see your student engaged in preparing for his or her future—just call or email to let me know you're coming.

I will also be communicating with you through phone calls, emails, and newsletters the students and I will send out on a monthly basis. The newsletters will keep you informed about what we are studying and general classroom news. I also have a class website available at _____. On the website you can find homework assignments and other day-to-day news. I will try to keep the site as current as possible.

Once again, I want to say how much I am looking forward to working with your child and with you this coming year.

Sincerely,

Preparing Your Classroom for a Substitute Teacher

Michelle Bounds

This item is included to help teachers better prepare for substitute teachers. This form provides teachers with a means of consolidating information about the classroom into one easily accessible source. Once this form has been completed it should be kept in a file and not seen by students.

Substitute Information Sheet

Teacher's Name:

Room #:

Grade:

The following information can be found:

_____Lesson Plans:

_____Seating Chart(s):

_____Student Management Information:

_____Other:

Staff who can answer questions or assist:

Teacher:
Room #:

Teacher:
Room #:

Administrator in charge:

Name
Extension:

General Policies on:

Attention Signal:

Hall Passes:

Bathroom Privileges:

Breaks:

Library Passes:

Food/Drinks:

Gum/Candy:

Walkmans/Games:

Coats/Hats:

What to do if a student finishes work early:

Supplies:

Time Out Procedures:

Class Profile:

    Students who have special needs or health considerations:

    Students who leave the room at certain times and days of the week:

        Student:

        Time:

        Day(s):

        Going Where:

Teaching Assistants, Student Assistants, or Parent Volunteers:

    Name(s):

    Times:

    Day(s):

    Job Description(s):

Other Important Information:

Communicating
with the Community

This Overview Was Originally Developed
by Ginny Nimmo

A judicious learning community works best when it is supported by all members of the community—inside and outside of the school.

For *Judicious Discipline* to work well, all interested parties—parents, guardians, school administrators and the school's support staff—need to understand the concepts and be involved as partners in the implementation.

This section contains materials that teachers and administrators will find useful for helping parents, guardians, and other community members understand how implementing *Judicious Discipline* in schools and classrooms will help their students develop as citizens and be better able to make appropriate personal decisions.

Caregiver Information

As you begin a new philosophy of classroom discipline, such as *Judicious Discipline*, it is imperative that you inform the caregivers of your students about this new system of respect and responsibility. Many schools have found effective ways of achieving this objective. Some examples follow.

Many schools will set up an *information presentation* during an open house. This can be done by offering short presentations throughout the evening, or one at the beginning of the evening. Another idea would be to set aside a day and offer a short presentation before school, at noon, and in the evening. If doing a presentation of this kind, be sure to use some clear example of how this will be/has been introduced to students. For instance, you might use one of the lessons included in Part Two of this volume. It is often helpful to have the students assist you by having them describe their rights and responsibilities.

Several school districts have begun using *pre-conferences* before the start of the school year. If this is done, then having a one page handout about *Judicious Discipline* available to parents is important, and explanations can be done at that time if caregivers are not familiar with the philosophy. An example of such a handout is the "Overview for Caregivers" which follows next in this section.

It is a great idea to make a *video* of an opening presentation to students. This video can be sent home for caregivers to view, and is also a good tool than can be used when new students enter the building. This should be short, 15 to 20 minutes, making use of the school principal, counselor and other support personnel.

Another way to get information to caregivers over the course of a year's time is the use of the *school newsletter*. Explaining one aspect of *Judicious Discipline* each month, and then eventually also introducing *Judicious Parenting* is very helpful to caregivers. Such newsletter articles are not only a good means of discussion with students and their caregivers, but also remind the staff each month that this is the model you are trying to provide students. Examples of such newsletter articles follow in this section.

Caregivers generally appreciate the concepts of *Judicious Discipline* once they understand them. Misunderstandings occur when we, as educators, do not take the time to communicate this philosophy to our students' caregivers. Using one of these methods may be a beginning of creating a respectful community where caregivers can also feel that they are heard.

An Overview of *Judicious Discipline* for Caregivers

(Please work with translators so that this letter to caregivers will be in the primary languages spoken in the homes of students.)

Judicious Discipline is a management framework which combines sound educational practices, professional ethics, and students' constitutional rights and responsibilities. We all want for our students to become responsible citizens, and this framework educates them about their personal freedoms and how those freedoms are always balanced with social responsibilities. In short, the *Judicious Discipline* framework teaches them about and allows them to practice citizenship every day in school.

In school, the rights on which we focus are three:

First Amendment: freedom of expression
Fourth Amendment: protection against search and seizure
Fourteenth Amendment: right to due process

Once we have discussed these with the students, we help them understand that although their rights are very important, their individual rights do not "supersede the needs of the whole." In constitutional law there are times when an individual's rights can be limited, and they are called "compelling state interests." These interests form the basis for our school's rules and help to ensure the health, safety and welfare of all students. There are only four compelling state interests and they are the basis for all the rules we have in our school.

1. Protect against property loss or damage.

2. Be a responsible learner—work toward the educational purpose in each task.

3. Act in a healthy and safe manner—this includes issues of emotional health.

4. Respect the rights of others—guard against the disruption of the educational process.

Teaching rights and responsibilities through *Judicious Discipline* helps us focus on what students need to learn in any given behavioral or academic situation. In order to help them understand expectations, we may need to use consequences. Judicious consequences always consider the self-worth and academic success of each child, and move away from a punishment to a "recover and learn from our mistakes" approach.

Caregivers may want more information about the school personnel, in addition to teachers, who are used to help students develop their responsibilities. These may include the school principal, resource room teacher, school nurse, school counselor, school psychologist, or co-location worker. These people are available to meet with you when interests or needs arise.

For more information regarding *Judicious Discipline* you are invited to visit our school library and check out one or more of the books listed below.

Judicious Discipline (6th Ed.), by Forrest Gathercoal, Caddo Gap Press, 2004.

Practicing Judicious Discipline (4th Ed.), edited by Barbara McEwan, Caddo Gap Press, 2007.

Judicious Parenting, by Forrest Gathercoal, Caddo Gap Press, 1992.

Newsletters Featuring *Judicious Discipline*

The following items are newsletter articles all originally contributed by Ginny Nimmo. The names of the schools change from article to article because the original author was drawing from a school district's efforts to keep caregivers informed about their shared approach to management.

Sample Newsletter Article I:
Introducing Judicious Discipline

> **judicious**...1. having or exercising sound judgment...2. directed or governed by sound, usually, dispassionate judgment; characterized by discretion... **syn.** see **wise.** —*Webster's Third New International Dictionary*

discipline...1. a branch of knowledge or learning...2. training that develops self-control, character, or orderliness and efficiency... 3. self-control or orderly conduct...4. a system of rules... 5. treatment that corrects. —*Webster's New World Dictionary*

Washington Elementary is beginning its third year using the philosophy of *Judicious Discipline* in the 4/5 multi-age and the second year in the 2/3 level. This philosophy was developed by Forrest Gathercoal of Oregon State University. It is a democratic approach for fostering respectful and responsible learning communities.

In *Judicious Discipline* we believe that all students deserve the opportunity for an equal education, but that opportunity must be balanced with responsibilities that help all students develop a sense of repect for the needs of others as well as self-discipline. *Judicious Discipline* is a philosophy which is a combination of sound educational principles and constitutional law, designed to teach students how to be responsible citizens in our democratic society.

As educators (and as caregivers, you are your child's first and most important teacher), we want to work cooperatively with you, in helping students recover and learn from their mistakes. We must keep in mind that our children are not finished yet, but are in the process of growing to adulthood. Since we want our children to grow to be responsible citizens, we must work together to help our students learn to make choices that help themselves and others live respectfully and responsibly.

In the weeks and months to come, you will have an opportunity to learn more about the concepts of *Judicious Discipline*. These concepts are applicable to children from the time they can learn to talk, through adulthood. In this newsletter, I will be sharing more about the constitutional rights and responsibilities we are discussing with all our students, as well as how you, as caregivers, can support your child's effort to develop as a caring and respectful member of our society. As always, I invite your emails, phone calls and face to face conferences to discuss any concerns or questions you might have regarding our school's approach to management.

During open house, many parents displayed an interest in learning more about *Judicious Discipline*. They reported students coming home and informing them that as students, they "had rights"! It is true that the philosophy of *Judicious Discipline* is one that teaches students the "rights" guaranteed to them in the United States Constitution. Specifically, we teach the right to freedom of expression (First Amendment), the right to protect against search and seizure (Fourth Amendment), and the right to due process (Fourteenth Amendment).

We teach students that although we live in a "free" society where we are given these rights, it does *not* give them the license to do as they please. Students are shown that there must be a "balance" in order to maintain each individual's rights.

We use what are called the four compelling state interests. Our society and our school uses this language to limit individual freedoms for the safety and welfare of society. At Garfield, we have chosen to adopt these as our school and classroom responsibilities. They are as follows:

1. Respect property—protect against property loss and damage.

2. Be a responsible learner—work toward the educational purpose in each task.

3. Act in a healthy and safe manner—includes physical and emotional safety issues.

4. Respect the rights of others—guard against the disruption of the educational process.

Through the use of compelling state interests, we help students understand that the balance between their rights and responsibilities is critical. An example of how we might limit a First Amendment right would be to tell a student it is not okay to use "freedom of expression" to put down another student, thus harming that student's emotional health and safety.

276

Through the use of *Judicious Discipline*, we are trying to empower students to use their "rights," by keeping them in balance with everyone else's physical and emotional needs. We are emphasizing an atmosphere where students and adults are worthy of respect, and capable of being responsible for themselves and each other. Each month another component of *Judicious Discipline* will be shared with you in this newsletter, and in the months to come we will be printing specific ideas of how this can be adapted to your family. As always, I invite your emails, phone calls and face to face conferences to discuss any concerns or questions you might have regarding our school's approach to management.

Sample Newsletter Article III:
Time, Place, and Manner

As we enter into the new year, future newsletter articles will deal more with the concepts of using *Judicious Discipline* in our family. In previous newsletter articles I have briefly mentioned the concept of "Time, Place, and Manner" (TPM).

In a democracy, individual actions can be limited by the government to a reasonable "time, place, and manner." We find ourselves using TPM in so many ways and for so many situations. It can work as an organizer for groups, such as in our classrooms, or with individuals within small groups, or in families.

For instance this is an example of how we might use TPM in a Physical Education class. Let's say a student is upset about something and throws a volleyball as hard as she can into someone's body. After checking to be sure of the physical and emotional needs of the student who has been hit, the next step is to have a discussion with the angry student. The intervening time can be used to let the angry student calm down in a quiet "time out" area. Talking with the student will include questions like "What is happening?" "I can see you are angry. What can you tell me about it?" After hearing the student's side of the issue and getting information you may need to act on (Did the other student do something that triggered the action?) you can go on to talk about "What is the appropriate manner that we should handle a

277

volleyball? Is there ever an appropriate time or place that someone might throw a ball very hard? If someone calls you a name, who are the people that can help you resolve the conflict? What is the appropriate manner to handle your anger?" This redirection is very important but it cannot be effective unless we have first heard the student's side of the situation.

After a discussion, there may still be consequences for the act, such as apology, or some type of restitution—such as helping the offended child, or it may be necessary to act as a mediator between the two students to help them resolve the conflict that led to this problem.

The concept of time, place, and manner is also very helpful in the family. When discussing responsibilities such as practicing an instrument, instead of getting into an argument about practice time, a parent might ask, "At what time today will you arrange to practice the piano. Will that affect someone else's need to practice, or use the room for something else?" Or, if your son or daughter is very insistent about doing something, and you don't like the way they are talking to you, you can respond with "What is the appropriate manner you could ask me about this, so that I might be more open to listening?" Another example might be a child who is choosing to leave his or her personal items all over the house. "Where in this house (what place) might it be okay to leave your things wherever you like?" "What can be done so that your things don't always end up by the front door, or in the living room?"

By using "time, place, and manner" we can teach our children their responsibilities, without always feeling like a nagging parent. TPM can help us to create an atmosphere of respect and communication.

Sample Newsletter Article IV:
Judicious Consequences

In the last newsletter, we looked at the concepts of "rights and responsibilities." Often, when a student is reminded of a responsibility, that is all we need to do to change that behavior. But what do we do if this particular area of responsibility is a constant concern, or if we feel we have done enough reminding—now we want the child to assume the responsibility themselves? This is when "judicious consequences" are needed.

Judicious consequences should be commensurate with the behavior we want to change and they should be compatible with the self-esteem and academic success of the student. We, as the adults, need to ask, "What needs to be learned?" and, "What needs to be done?" When those questions are used, often an appropriate consequence can be chosen. We should always include the child in the process of determining the consequence once we both understand what needs to be learned and what needs to be done. Because each child may need to learn something different (they are individuals, and to be fair, we must determine what they need to learn in this situation), the consequences will be individually chosen.

If a child continues to have difficulty with a responsibility at school, or exhibits a behavior that is of particular concern to us, we may communicate to you the child's caregiver through a behavior report. [Ed. note: There are two sample behavior reports included in Part III. Readers should feel free to use them as is or adapt them as necessary.] This allows you, as the caregiver, to work cooperatively with us to discuss this concern with your child. If your child brings home a behavior form, consider these questions:

1. What needs to be learned here?

2. What is my role as a guiding and responsible parent in resolving the problem?

3. Do I need more information about the events surrounding the problem?

4. What strategies can I use to get this child talking about and beginning to own the problem?

5. Once the problem is clearly defined, what needs to be done?

As caregivers , you are your child's first and most important teacher. As educators, we want to work cooperatively with you in helping students recover and learn from their mistakes. We all want our children to grow to be responsible citizens, so we must work together to help them to learn to accept responsibility, and move on to be more productive in their choices. In the newsletters to come, more issues regarding *Judicious Discipline* will be shared with you, including ways in which we, as adults, can be the responsible models for our own choices. As always, I invite your emails, phone calls and face to face conferences to discuss any concerns or questions you might have regarding our school's approach to management.

Sample Newsletter Article V:
Judicious Discipline *in the Family*

We have noticed that faculty, administrators, staff, and caregivers have a positive response to the concepts of *Judicious Discipline*. The students report that they also like the approach because they feel trusted and respected. It is exciting to use these concepts of mutual respect to help students see the importance of being responsible for themselves. Many caregivers have also requested information as to whether *Judicious Discipline* as a democratic method of dealing with their children's behavior is possible at home. For many years material has been used in parenting classes that closely fits with *Judicious Discipline*, but for success to occur, all family members must understand what a true democratic family is, and is not!

Living in a democratic family does not mean living in a permissive environment, nor does it mean that every decision is decided by a majority vote. In every democracy there is a need for good leadership, and in a family the leaders are the caregivers. In a democratic family the parent's role is to balance the rights of the individual with the welfare needs of all the others. The caregivers are not in the role of "boss," such as in autocratic systems, but rather leaders, who are wise and just. In order to create a family where children are respected, caregivers and children need to learn a new language—the language of civility.

When teaching your children about citizenship in a democratic society, it is important to help them better understand three basic values: freedom, justice, and equality.

280

Freedom does not mean we can do whatever we please. It does allow individuals to be themselves, but their actions must always be balanced with the needs and the welfare of others.

Justice deals with fairness, or due process. Justice provides us with the means by which we can be heard.

Equality gives us the problem of sharing burdens and benefits. "All people are created equal" does not mean we all possess the same abilities, interests or talents. Equality means getting an equal opportunity to succeed, keeping in mind the individual's needs.

This terminology is not meant to be a legal brief, but rather a means by which we can develop a language that is educational, as well as respectful. Now that you have the basic language, the next step will be to develop some family rules based on health and safety, legitimate family purpose, property loss and damage and serious disruption. Even in a democracy there are rules (laws). You are right! But we are running out of space for this month! Watch for next month's newsletter for family rules!

If this is frustrating, and you simply cannot wait, I invite your emails, phone calls and face to face conferences to discuss any concerns or questions you might have regarding our school's approach to management. In addition, you may want to consider purchasing the book, *Judicious Parenting*, by Forrest Gathercoal, published in 1992 by Caddo Gap Press. It is from this book that all of the information in this article has been taken.

Sample Newsletter Article VI:
Family Responsibilities

In last month's newsletter we learned that a democratic family structure does not mean a permissive structure, but rather that all members have rights that need to be balanced with the welfare of the others involved. This can be accomplished by developing family rules and experiences in which children feel there is an emphasis on personal freedoms, and then helping them make responsible decisions around those freedoms that carefully consider the interests and welfare of others.

For years, United States courts have been using four basic

state welfare arguments to maintain the balance between rights and responsibilities. These are called compelling state interests. These remind us that the needs of the majority are so strong that our individual rights may be limited or even denied to protect the common good. In schools, our decisions about student behavior are based on these four interests (as listed in previous newsletter articles). Theses same compelling state interests can be translated into family terms, and used as a means of teaching our children appropriate examples of behavior.

1. *Property loss or damage*—"Put your toys away when you are finished playing," "We sit on the furniture," "We need to fix something if it is broken, or get it repaired." Family discussions about the proper care and use of property help children learn the value of caring for property outside of the home. Consequences should include the concepts of restitution and apologies. Discussion about these issues before it occurs will help the child accept them when there is a problem.

2. *Threat to health and safety*—"Use a helmet when you ride your bike," "Dress appropriately for the weather," "Cover your mouth when you cough." When discussing issues of health and safety, help the child understand the respect for dangerous or unhealthy situations. Help children understand the natural, serious consequences for unsafe behavior. Also discuss how each family member may affect each other's emotional safety, and discuss the manner in which disputes can be settled.

3. *Serious disruption of the family community*—"Take your turn when someone is talking, let them finish their thought," "Call me if you go to a friend's house after school," "You need to put your clothes in the wash if you want it clean for school." More than anything, this area becomes a matter of good communication. Helping children understand appropriate methods of communication, and "rules" that are necessary if your family is going to function are all extremely important. More than anything, caregivers need to model these same behaviors—listen to children when they talk, call if they will be late, pick up their clothes and get them in the wash, etc. Discussion will focus on methods to communicate, as well as what are reasonable expectations.

4. *Legitimate family purpose*—This is the chance for your family to teach what is most important to you. "Sunday is a family day in our house," "There is no television on in our house until your homework is done," "Our family doesn't wear clothing with this type of language on it." It is a chance for you to teach your own family values, but in a way that helps them understand that in any environment (work or school) there are certain expectations placed on them. It reminds them that when they are in other settings, "Is this the way my caregivers would want me to act?" These are issues which must be discussed with children so that they understand the purpose of these "rules"—the history behind them. Family values such as cooperation, responsibility, work ethic, religious belief are a few examples. Consequences for not following legitimate family interests should be primarily educational and mentoring. Again, the most effective method is the model the caregivers provide in this area.

More ideas will be shared next month in the developing of rules, and the concept of family meetings. As always, I invite your emails, phone calls and face to face conferences to discuss any concerns or questions you might have regarding our school's approach to management. If you want to read more about these concepts, consider the book, *Judicious Parenting*, by Forrest Gathercoal, published by Caddo Gap Press.

Sample Newsletter Article VII:
More Ideas for the Family

In last month's newsletter, we discussed "Compelling Family Interests" and briefly those are:

1. Property loss and damage;
2. Threat to health and safety;
3. Serious disruption of the family community;
4. Legitimate family interests.

Remember, the compelling family interests are the framework as to how we can teach children to balance their freedoms with their responsibilities. These can also be the framework, or the principles used in developing family rules.

Rules need to be stated in a positive manner. Rather than saying, "Don't run in the house," an example might be, "We walk in the house, remember health and safety." By stating the rules giving the expected behavior, and adding the accompanying compelling family interest, you are helping the child to see that rules are for a reason—they are not arbitrary. It gives them the tools in handling themselves when they are not in your sight, or when they walk out of your home.

Have you ever had your child say to you, "You didn't tell me that was a rule!" Or, "I didn't know what you meant when you said ...."? When you state rules, and remind them of the compelling family interest, power struggles are often eliminated. Discussion can occur in a more positive vein, using language such as, "We need to remember to consider the needs and welfare of others when...." A marvelous vehicle for these discussions can be family meetings.

Family meetings are a very proactive means for dealing with the many issues that come up when living together in a family. In order for these to work well, caregivers must be willing to take the time to demonstrate a respectful model as to how to handle conflict, as well as to celebrate! It is also a wonderful chance to demonstrate the concept of "due process" in a family setting. Next month's newsletter will give an outline for a family meeting, as well as numerous ideas for discussion items.

Sample Newsletter Article VIII:
The Family Meeting

In previous newsletter articles I have discussed the many components of *Judicious Discipline*. Another proactive component to the "judicious" parenting is the family meeting. It is a time when the feelings and opinions of children, as well as those of the caregivers, can be heard and respected. Concerns can be voiced, and consensus can be formed on issues that are day-to-day matters, as well as those which require more long-range planning.

The first meeting should be set up to describe a democratic family. [Ed. note: Families might want to base some of the process of the sample lesson plan for setting up class meetings that is included in the last section of Part II.] This would be an ideal time to discuss constitutional rights and responsibilities. A discussion should occur as to how "compelling family interests" are in order to provide for the welfare of the majority—to create "family citizens."

A possible outline for this discussion might be:

1. Talk about the principles of civility and family values, and how they can be a basis for family rules and consequences.

2. Talk about the ways Freedom, Justice and Equality might be interpreted in your home. Since children do not have constitutional rights in the home, you can be very clear that this is how your family will interpret the concepts. Discuss the four compelling state interests, and how rights can be limited or denied if the family balance is tipped.

3. Discuss your ideals about how you view the responsibilities and ethics of parenting.

4. Explain that the majority does not always rule—issues are best resolved by balancing the needs and interest of each family member, and often it is the parent's authority to regulate the children's rights to a reasonable time, place and manner.

After the initial meeting, agendas can be used (kept on the refrigerator or other posting area), and both caregivers and children can write issues they want to remember to discuss at the next family meeting. Some meetings can be set at regular times; others may need to be impromptu, for immediate concerns.

Finally, remember to celebrate the decisions you make, and thank your children for the many responsible decisions they make.

Acknowledgments
of Contributing Authors
and Additional Resources

This 4th edition of *Practicing Judicious Discipline* reflects my good fortune to be working at the University of Hawaii, Manoa, and the work of people I feel fortunate to call colleagues. This edition also contains some new and some revised works. They are listed below.

Part One
   Nancy Busse, School Administrator, Minnesota
   Forrest Gathercoal, Professor Emeritus, Oregon State
      University
   Paul Gathercoal, Professor, California Lutheran University
   Donna Grace, Associate Professor, University of Hawai'i
   Jennifer Herring, Assistant Specialist, University of Hawai'i
   Younghee Kim, Associate Professor, Southern Oregon
      University
   Julie Petersen, Teacher, Minnesota
   A. Ku'ulei Serna, Assistant Professor, University of Hawai'i
   Bonnie Tinker, Director of Love Makes a Family, Portland,
      Oregon

Part Two (In addition to those already listed above)
   Primary
   Margaret Abbott, Retired School Administrator, Oregon

287

Bobbie Martel, Instructor, Leeward Community College, O'ahu

Tammy Tasker, Doctoral Student, University of Washington

Intermediate
Karen Higgins, Associate Professor, Oregon State University

Middle Level
Jane Richards, Teacher, New York
Betty Powers, Teacher, New York

Secondary
Richard Newman, Teacher, Oregon
Juanita Weber-Shirk, Teacher, New York

Part Three
Heidi Weismuller, Teacher, New York
Michelle Bounds, Teacher, Oregon
Ginny Nimmo, Special Education Coordinator, Mankato, Minnesota

I am very grateful for the time and energy these colleagues gave to improve and update this edition of *Practicing Judicious Discipline*. If you would like more information about *Judicious Discipline* workshops or would like to communicate with those of us working to continue the development of this framework, you can visit the following websites.

The Judicious Discipline Home Page
http://www.dock.net/gathercoal/judicious_discipline.html
or type Judicious Discipline into your favorite browser

You can find me at www.eduquestlearning.com or email me at landau@eduquestlearning.com. I will look forward to chatting with you.

As we say in Hawai'i – Mahalo (Thank you)

—Barbara Landau